POLITICS, LIES AND CONSPIRACY THEORIES

Politics, Lies and Conspiracy Theories: A Cognitive Linguistic Perspective shows how language influences mechanisms of cognition, perception, and belief, and by extension its power to manipulate thoughts and beliefs.

This exciting and original work is the first to apply cognitive linguistics to the analysis of political lies and conspiracy theories, both of which have flourished in the internet age and which many argue are threatening democracy. It unravels the verbal mechanisms that make these "different truths" so effective and proliferative, dissecting the verbal structures (metaphor, irony, connotative implications, etc.) of a variety of real-life cases concerning politicians, conspiracy theorists, and influencers. Marcel Danesi goes on to demonstrate how these linguistic structures "switch on" or "switch off" alternative mind worlds.

This book is essential reading for students of cognitive linguistics and will enrich the studies of any student or researcher in language and linguistics more broadly, as well as discourse analysis, rhetoric, or political science.

Marcel Danesi is a Professor Emeritus of linguistic anthropology and semiotics at the University of Toronto.

POLITICS, LIES AND CONSPIRACY THEORIES

A Cognitive Linguistic Perspective

Marcel Danesi

Routledge
Taylor & Francis Group

LONDON AND NEW YORK

Designed cover image: © Getty Images | andy dauer

First published 2023
by Routledge
4 Park Square, Milton Park, Abingdon, Oxon OX14 4RN

and by Routledge
605 Third Avenue, New York, NY 10158

Routledge is an imprint of the Taylor & Francis Group, an informa business

British Library Cataloguing-in-Publication Data
A catalogue record for this book is available from the British Library

ISBN: 978-1-032-39313-1 (hbk)
ISBN: 978-1-032-39312-4 (pbk)
ISBN: 978-1-003-34914-3 (ebk)

DOI: 10.4324/9781003349143

Typeset in Bembo
by MPS Limited, Dehradun

CONTENTS

PREFACE

The premise on which this book is based is that language can be manipulated by clever, nefarious politically motivated actors to manufacture thoughts and beliefs that they can use for self-serving purposes. This is not a new idea, of course, having been debated and discussed across time, from Plato's dialogue *Gorgias*, in which the argument is made that rhetorical discourse can be used for nefarious purposes (Plato 1994), to George Orwell's powerful 1949 novel, *Nineteen Eighty-Four*, where lying is seen as the main strategy of politically manipulative discourse. Given the ubiquity of such discourse today, spreading globally through cyberspace, it is becoming critical to decipher and expose the underlying conceptual and verbal mechanisms that undergird such discourse, given that it is becoming a powerful factor in generating political and social instability worldwide. The main approach taken here is the so-called *cognitive linguistic* one, which has actually been applied to the study of political discourse in general, but rarely in a comprehensive way to the examination of the cognitive-linguitic sources of lies and conspiracy theories. That is the goal of this book.

The study of the relation between language and politics has received considerable attention from linguists (for example, Shapiro 1984; Osgood 1968; Joseph 2006; Yu 2013). In a growing number of works in this field, the role of metaphor is also examined. For instance, the book by Andreas Musolff (2004), *Metaphor and Political Discourse*, looks at the "metaphorical scenarios" that political actors in the United Kingdom and Germany have utilized to portray otherness in both positive and negative ways; the collection of studies, edited by Terrell Carver and Jernej Pikalo, *Political Language and Metaphor* (2008), contains situation-specific studies of the role of metaphor in politics, showing how various methodological approaches can be used to understand its use in political persuasion; and the collection edited by Michael Hanne, William D. Crano, Jeffery Scott Mio, *Warring with Words: Narrative and Metaphor in Politics* (2014), deals with examples of the role played by metaphorical cognition in the constitution of various polities across societies. But the scholar who has carved out the cognitive linguistic approach to metaphor in politics concretely is George Lakoff, with books such as *Don't Think of an Elephant* (2004) and *Moral Politics: How Liberals and Conservatives Think* (2016a). As is well known, it is Lakoff himself who developed the theory of conceptual metaphors as the cognitive mechanisms that undergird abstract thought. Lakoff looked at the kinds of metaphors that characterize the different kinds of political discourses on the right and left of the political spectrum in America.

But Lakoff's approach to political lies is exceptional; in fact, a review of works in this field, by Otieno, Owino, and Attyang (2016), indicates that cognitive linguistic analysis has been used only sporadically, overall, as a tool for decoding the psychological-linguistic sources of lies and conspiracy theories. Interestingly, from Aristotle to Cicero, the ancient rhetoricians understood the power of metaphor to persuade or dissuade people to act in certain ways (Gallagher 2001). It is a self-contained linguistic medium that seems to get people to accept the orator's point of view unwittingly (Scott Mio 1996, Bougher 2012). A classic example taken from American politics is Franklin Roosevelt's 1933 inaugural address, where he used the metaphor of an *army* as a means to persuade people to *fight* together to beat the Depression: "I assume unhesitatingly the leadership of the great army of our people dedicated to a disciplined attack upon our common problems." In his 1993 inaugural address, Bill Clinton deployed the metaphor of the season of *spring* to convey the sense that he was elected to bring about rebirth and regeneration: "Yes, you, my fellow Americans, have forced the spring. Now we must do the work the season demands." As such addresses show, their persuasiveness is based on a "central governing metaphor" upon which the orator implants their plea to action.

Because of its persuasive qualities, metaphor has been used systematically by tyrants and dictators, for nefarious reasons. The goal of this book is to look specifically at the kind of metaphorical discourse that such political actors have used and continue to use, utilizing the tools of cognitive linguistics in a general, non-technical way. The core perspective of this school of linguistic analysis is that metaphor is a trace of how the brain processes meaning. If so, then its main ideas can be used to decode political lies and conspiracy theories in a significant way, which is crucial today given the crystallization of the "global discourse of lying" on social media and other digital spaces, affecting the stability of the world. A subtext of this book is that lies and conspiracy theories do not go away by themselves, given that they tend to become embedded in groupthink; for this reason, it is critical to decode them and expose them for what they are—rhetorical constructions manufactured to gain consent.

This book is intended partly as a textbook on how lies, deceptions, and conspiracy theories can be deconstructed with the tools of cognitive linguistics. I am aware, of course, that this approach is not accepted universally by linguists. However, I believe that it can be used nonetheless as a practical tool for decomposing mendacious speech into its conceptual forms, no matter what particular school of analysis to which one subscribes. I do not assume any background technical knowledge on the part of the reader. I will describe and illustrate all technical aspects at the appropriate places in this book. Chapter 1 is designed to give an overview of lies, deception, and conspiracy theories; Chapter 2 then focuses on how to decode political lying, while Chapter 3 will focus on how conceptual metaphors undergird conspiracy theories. Chapter 4 then looks at the topic of fake news and how it engenders false beliefs. Chapter 5 discusses the notion of mythic lies—lies shaped by unconscious mythic narratives. Chapter 6 deals with the media used to spread lies and conspiracy theories, and how these reinforce and even shape them. Chapter 7 presents an overview of the subject matter of this book, so as to complete the analytical picture by tying loose theoretical threads together.

The underlying perspective that I have adopted for this book is encapsulated in a well-known anecdote connected to the Polish-American scholar, Alfred Korzybski (cited in Derks and Hollander 1996: 58). As he was giving a lecture to a group of students one day, at a certain point Korzybski stopped talking and took out a small packet of biscuits from his briefcase, telling the class that he just had to eat something due to a sudden attack of hunger. Showing politeness, he offered the biscuits to students seated in the front row, some of whom took one, eating it with apparent gusto. As they were digesting the biscuits, Korzybski remarked, "Nice biscuit, don't you think?" Then he tore off the wrapper around the packet, revealing the original packaging, which showed the picture of a dog's head and the label, *Dog Biscuits*. The students became visibly upset—two of them even ran out of the room to a toilet to vomit. Korzybski then turned to the rest of the class and uttered: "You see, I have just demonstrated that people don't just eat food, but also words, and that the taste of the former is often outdone by the taste of the latter." The objective of Korzybski's little game was to show that each time we use language, reactions, psychological and physical, can be "switched on" (to use a metaphor). The students showed no adverse effects at first by eating the cookies, thinking that they were intended for human consumption. These were evoked when they were shown the *Dog Biscuits* label, which re-directed their minds to a different referential frame (eating dog food), producing negative effects as a consequence.

A lie, like a label in this anecdote, will condition reactions and even affect the body. Once a lie is accepted and believed, the truth no longer matters. Labeling certain groups as "animals," "pigs," "monkeys," and the like, which are all animal metaphors intended to evoke images of aversion in people's minds, have the same ability to turn people's "mind switch" on manipulatively. The book ends by offering tentative suggestions of how that switch might be turned back off.

Marcel Danesi
University of Toronto, 2022

1

LIES AND CONSPIRACY THEORIES

Prologue

A classic case of what happens when facts are manipulated and lies are concocted about someone is the so-called Dreyfus Affair. In 1894, a French army officer named Alfred Dreyfus was accused falsely of providing military secrets to Germany. His trial, conviction, and imprisonment sparked a major political crisis in France. The miscarriage of justice has been attributed to antisemitism, given the fact that Dreyfus was Jewish. So, no matter what evidence was brought forward in his defense, and how logical the arguments were in his favor, reason and truth yielded to false beliefs and hidden prejudices. As was later discovered, the incriminating evidence was fabricated by an army major, Charles Esterhazy. Dreyfus was given a second trial in 1899, but he was again declared guilty of treason, despite evidence of his innocence. He was finally exonerated in 1906. But not everyone in France accepted that Dreyfus was innocent even after acquittal. It became a political game metaphor—those who supported Dreyfus were seen as having "won," while the side that did not accept the verdict, was perceived as having "lost." At the time, Jewish people were struggling for full inclusion, while fanatical nationalists were attacking them as aliens and traitors. During the trial, riots erupted across France, as antisemitic groups used it to stir up racial hatred because the lie exacerbated divisions in the country that were traceable back to the French Revolution.

This case showed three things at once: (1) when a lie that has a political or racial bias built into it is perpetrated, it can stoke hatred that will hardly ever dissipate, no matter the facts; (2) this kind of lie is destructive of social harmony; (3) it provides an opportunity for politically motivated individuals to organize themselves around a cause. The Dreyfus Affair is just one example of how people are susceptible and vulnerable to lies that tap into unconscious prejudicial beliefs and biases. Many such

DOI: 10.4324/9781003349143-1

episodes have occurred throughout history, suggesting that reason, justice, and even social sanity are often at risk in the face of lies and false conspiracy theories, such as the one perpetrated by Esterhazy. As the political theorist Hannah Arendt (1978) once stated, the reason why lies have such deleterious effects is "not that you believe the lies, but rather that nobody believes anything any longer." Before discussing politically motivated lies and conspiracy theories in greater detail in subsequent chapters, the purpose of this chapter is to provide a schematic overview of the nature of lies and conspiracy theories, including how they are used to instill and propagate hatred of others. The view of metaphorical language as powerful persuasive speech, as argued by philosophers such as Hobbes and Nietzsche, will conclude the chapter.

Lies and Lying

Lying is something everyone does, every day, arguably because it is at times necessary to maintain fluid social relations, or else as a self-defense strategy. Early in life, children come to realize that lying can help them avoid negative reactions, evade trouble, circumvent hurtful truths, or obtain something desired by duplicity. Since no one has ever taught any child to lie, it is logical to deduce that lying may be an innate trait, emerging during infancy. According to some evolutionary psychologists, it may well be a sign of intelligence, connected with survival, given that it reveals a purposive way to gain some advantage or to avoid adversity. Analogs to lying exist in other species, but these hardly come close to the type of deception of which humans are capable. One of these is camouflage, which enables certain species to blend in with their surroundings as a tactic of disguise. This is an instinctive form that does not involve intentionality. Primates, however, may show a form of intentional deception. A chimp foraging for food might pretend not to have noticed the food, in order to avoid alerting other chimps in its group as to its location. But even such calculated behavior does not match the type of deception that human lying reveals. The reason is that language is required to carry it off along with a kind of "mind-reading" ability. As Richard Wright (1995) observes in *The Moral Animal*, lying involves the ability to understand what is in someone else's mind and then to use it to deceive that person through linguistic fabrications. Whatever the psychological-evolutionary truth of the matter, there is little doubt that the ability to intentionally manipulate someone else's mind through the use of untruths is unique to humans.

The presence of lying in human affairs has fascinated us since the beginning of time, given that it appears intrinsically in origin stories across the world. For instance, the fall of humanity from Paradise, as recounted in the Bible, is brought about by a temptation instigated by the first master liar of the world, Lucifer, who deceived not only Adam and Eve, but also the other angels with his duplicity and deviousness. John 8:44 depicts him as follows: "He was a murderer from the beginning, and abode not in the truth, because there is no truth in him; he is a liar, and the father of it." The story shows an understanding that humans have always been vulnerable to lies—a vulnerability that can be used for manipulative purposes as the Genesis story implies. As neuroscientist Sam Harris (2011: 23) has so aptly remarked, from the dawn of history, humans have come to realize that lying is an intentional act that works psychologically because we almost always "expect honest communication." As Harris (2011: 24) goes on to observe, some types of lies are particularly destructive of honest dialogue and even of mental balance, given that they might activate belief mechanisms that are not grounded in reality: "People lie so that others will form beliefs that are not true. The more consequential the beliefs—that is, the more a person's well-being depends upon a correct under-standing of the world—the more consequential the lie."

For the present purposes, lies can be assigned to two broad categories, known colloquially as "white" and "black." The former are lies told typically to avoid offending or hurting someone's feelings, to skirt around troubles, to prevaricate about frustrations and setbacks, to avoid reprobation, and to equivocate in order to avoid negative consequences, as when children say that they have done their homework even though this is not true. In a classic psychological study of white lies, DePaulo et al. (1996) classified them into three subcategories: (1) "self-oriented," which are lies devised to protect or enhance self-interests, including shelter from embarrassment, loss of face, loss of status, and so on; (2) "other-oriented," which are fabricated to protect or enhance someone else, including when parents brag about the skills of their children without any substance to the claims; and (3) "outright falsehoods," which are intended for some self-serving reason or else to bring harm upon someone else. The latter category overlaps considerably with the generic category of "black lies," which seem to have no purpose other than to harm someone, as the Dreyfus Affair revealed. To extend the color metaphor, black lies are part of a "dark" verbal art, involving a malicious deployment of duplicitous linguistic strategies, including fab-rication, falsification, deceit, deception, and exaggeration, whose sole purpose is to instigate emotional damage. It is this art that is of direct concern in this book. It is little wonder that Lucifer was called the "Prince of Darkness" by poet John Milton in his 1652 epic poem *Paradise Lost.*

Lies have been studied broadly within linguistics, as mentioned in the preface. The definition of lying that emerges generally from the field is that of a speech act that denies referential truth to words, violating British philosopher Paul Grice's maxims (1975, 1989), such as the implicit maxim of relevance, by which inter-locutors assume that anything spoken is intended to be pertinent (whether it is true or not). In other words, we assume that what someone says in a communicative interaction is relevant and thus truthful—unless revealed to be otherwise. This maxim describes the "default" condition for entering into any conversation. A lie works, therefore, if it is presented as relevant information. A consummate liar knows how to take advantage of this kind of interactional naïveté by manipulating it for some self-serving purpose. Grice's relevance maxim reflects our overall ex-pectation that, under normal circumstances, communication is part of ethical behavior. Lies violate this maxim.

To achieve their effect, lies distort the linkage between words, their referents, and their meanings. And this has direct effects on mind states and even behavior. Recall the Korzybski anecdote described in the preface. The gist of his game was to show that words link the mind to referential domains. Like the dog biscuit label, a lie can be seen as manipulating the link in clever ways. The results of this manipulation are hardly neutral, as we saw with the game—they bring about cognitive and behavioral consequences. This can be called the "Korzybski effect" for the sake of convenience—an effect that will be discussed throughout this book.

The master liar knows how to produce this effect, deploying it to deceive people into believing something that is not true, allowing him to forge allies and alliances and to offset opponents, who might fear his ability to destroy them via lies, as evidenced dramatically by the Dreyfus Affair and similar historical episodes—it is primarily historically powerful men who have utilized lying in this way, hence the use of the masculine pronoun throughout this book. This art of the political lie was described in a detailed fashion by Machiavelli in his 1532 book, *The Prince*, in which he advises rulers on how to acquire power by both ethical and unethical methods. It is the latter, Machiavelli suggests, that work best for the simple reason that people are drawn in by big lies, prefiguring this notion long before it came to be deployed by master liars such as Hitler and Stalin. In order for people to accept a big political lie, the liar must perpetrate a scenario that is so distortional of the truth that it would defy common sense to envision it as deceit. Moreover, to ensure that it is accepted as truth, the lie must be repeated frequently and never retracted, even in the face of contrary evidence or counterarguments. As Hitler (1925) perceptively realized, in Machiavellian style, if a lie is colossal and repeated over and over it becomes believable simply because people would think that no one "could have the impudence to distort the truth so infamously." As Socrates observed (in Plato 2022): "Whenever, therefore, people are deceived and form opinions wide of the truth, it is clear that the error has slid into their minds through the medium of certain resemblances to that truth".

Aware of the power of lies to influence human affairs destructively, the early Christian theologian, Augustine of Hippo, devoted two early treatises to this topic—*De mandacio* and *Contra mendacio*, published in English in one volume, *On Lying* (Augustine 1994; see Hermanowicz 2018). Augustine starts, actually, by emphasizing that lying can be used for good, such as saving someone from a wrongful fate, remarking that in such cases it is "praiseworthy to tell a lie" (Augustine 1994: 457). Modern examples of this occurred during the Holocaust, when people in countries such as Poland and Italy would lie to German officers about hiding Jewish people in their homes, or else create cover stories for them. Perhaps the best-known case of this occurred in the Netherlands, when, on August 4, 1944, after months in hiding, the Gestapo had learned about the hiding place of Jewish families from an anonymous tipster. This included the Frank family, whose daughter Anne Frank wrote a diary that documented the hardship faced by the Jews during the Nazi regime. On that day, the Gestapo knocked on the door where the Franks were living. A citizen named Miep Gies worked in the building at the time of the raid and avoided arrest because the officer was from her native Vienna and felt sympathy for her. When asked if there were Jews in the house, Giep responded by denying their presence. Augustine also presents the common situation when one may choose not to tell the truth to a gravely sick person, for fear that the person's health would worsen if we told them the truth. On the other hand, he strongly condemns the type of lie that "consists of speaking a falsehood with the intention of deceiving" (Augustine 1994: 477), emphasizing that "there is a difference between lying and being a liar;" that is, someone "may tell a lie unwittingly; but a liar loves to lie, and inhabits in his mind the delight of lying" (Augustine 1994: 477).

Perhaps no other book has been as effective in portraying the deleterious effects of mind control brought about by politically motivated lying and deception than George Orwell's novel, *Nineteen Eighty-Four* (1949). As the following excerpt shows, Orwell despised such lying because of its ability to indoctrinate people by impelling them to accept conflicting beliefs as truth, often at odds with their own memory or sense of reality (Orwell 1949: 44–45):

> To know and not to know, to be conscious of complete truthfulness while telling carefully constructed lies, to hold simultaneously two opinions which cancelled out, knowing them to be contradictory and believing in both of them, to use logic against logic, to repudiate morality while laying claim to it, to believe that democracy was impossible and that the Party was the guardian of democracy, to forget whatever it was necessary to forget, then to draw it back into memory again at the moment when it was needed, and then promptly to forget it again: and above all, to apply the same process to the process itself. That was the ultimate subtlety: consciously to induce unconsciousness, and then, once again, to become unconscious of the act of hypnosis you had just performed.

The statement that lying is hypnotic is not unlike Korzybski's demonstration that a single word label can induce a reaction that affects the body and mind simultaneously. Orwell saw the source of that reaction as connected to the unconscious effects of what he called "doublethink," whereby the meaning of words is designed to be intentionally ambiguous. He called the language that generated doublethink, "Newspeak," rephrased subsequently as "doublespeak." As media analyst Edward S. Herman has cogently argued, the principal feature of doublespeak is its skillful utilization of lying (Herman 1992: 3):

> What is really important in the world of doublespeak is the ability to lie, whether knowingly or unconsciously, and to get away with it; and the ability to use lies and choose and shape facts selectively, blocking out those that don't fit an agenda or program.

Doublethink can be characterized as a mind-state that simultaneously accepts contradictory beliefs or ideas as being both plausible. Orwell explains that while it may appear absurd at first, by constant usage doublespeak gains a form of cogency that users feel is just as valid as any form of discourse. It is this cogency that is exploited by totalitarian states, allowing Big Brother to exact conformity among the populace. The following excerpt from a speech given by Stalin to the 16th Congress of the Russian Communist Party in 1930 encapsulates the political manipulation underlying the doublespeak strategy perfectly (cited in Evans 1993: 39):

> We are for the withering away of the state, and at the same time we stand for the strengthening of the dictatorship, which represents the most powerful and mighty of all forms of the state which have existed up to the present day. The highest development of the power of the state, with the object of preparing the conditions of the withering away of the state: that is the Marxist formula. Is it "contradictory?" Yes, it is "contradictory." But this contradiction is a living thing and wholly reflects the Marxist dialectic.

During a speech he gave in Kansas City in July of 2018, the ex-American President Donald Trump made the following doublespeak statement: "What you are seeing and what you are reading, is not happening." This is taken right out of the Orwellian playbook on mind control: "The party told you to reject the evidence of your eyes and ears. It was their final, most essential command" (Orwell 1949: 23). As Trump seemingly understood, the doublespeak strategy allowed him to assign truth to himself—no other sources can be trusted since they are "enemies of the people," an expression that originated, not surprisingly, with Stalin. Trump employed the strategy of the "big lie" whereby he claimed falsely that his reelection in 2020 was stolen from him by duplicitous actors in what he called the "deep state." His tactic instilled a doublethink form of credulity among his most fervent followers, who accepted his lie as the truth, juxtaposing it against what they were "seeing and reading" in the mainstream media, as he had warned in his 2018 speech.

The notion of the big lie as a master political strategy traces its origin to Hitler's *Mein Kampf*. In its psychological profile of the Nazi dictator, the Office of Strategic Services (a US intelligence agency during World War II), described Hitler's use of the big lie strategy as follows (in Langer 1972):

> His primary rules were: never allow the public to cool off; never admit a fault or wrong; never concede that there may be some good in your enemy; never leave room for alternatives; never accept blame; concentrate on one enemy at a time and blame him for everything that goes wrong; people will believe a big lie sooner than a little one; and if you repeat it frequently enough people will sooner or later believe it.

Hitler may have intuitively understood that the strategy affects brain functioning, corroborated subsequently by neuroscience. In her 2004 book, *Brainwashing: The Science of Thought Control*, neuroscientist Kathleen Taylor described how people under the influence of big lies develop more rigid neural pathways, showing signs of difficulty in rethinking situations. Clearly, such lying is not just a form of duplicitous discourse that violates Grice's maxims, but mind-altering speech that destroys what William Bateson (1972) called the "ecology of mind." Especially critical in this scenario is metaphor since it creates, by its very nature, meaning through linkage (as will be discussed); and when this linkage is twisted by turning it into a big lie, the results are deleterious neurologically. As Bateson (1972) realized, metaphor constitutes the "whole fabric of mental interconnections," and once these are manipulated, the fabric itself will come apart.

The term *Machiavellian intelligence* was introduced by biologist Frans de Waals in his 1982 book, *Chimpanzee Politics*, in which he quotes Machiavelli to support his theory that lying emerged in human evolution to allow humans to engage advantageously within social groups—the more one is able to lie strategically the more psychological advantage one has over someone else. The evidence used to support this theory is the emergence of such verbal behavior in childhood (Byrne 1995, Livingstone 2002, Gavrilets and Vose 2006). But this line of argument misses a key aspect of human nature—*choice*—which Augustine called free will in his treatise, *On Free Choice of the Will* (written around 388 CE, see Augustine 1964). It is the intent to mislead or deceive that is at play in lying, argues Augustine. So, whatever the truth about the origins of lying in humans, there is little doubt that its use has hardly enhanced survival; rather, it has constantly put it at risk, given the consequences that it brings about.

Lies and Hate Speech

As the Dreyfus case made clear, politically motivated lies can, and often do, stimulate hatred of others. Lying and hate speech are two sides of the same malevolent coin—that is, when lies are intended to generate hate, harmful behaviors tend to result, including violence against the target individual or groups. While the verbal details may vary, the subtext to hate speech has been a constant one across time—others (foreigners) pose threats to the status quo and so any action against them is seen as necessary and thus justifiable.

The intent of such speech is, in effect, to attack those who do not belong to the mainstream (racial minorities, people of different sexual orientations, and so on) using dehumanizing language, nonverbal representations (cartoons, caricatures, etc.), and conspiracy narratives. Over time, the words, images, and stories accumulate in the unconscious mind to engender what journalist Walter Lippmann (1922) called "simplified pictures in the mind" of others that become deeply rooted in a given culture, influencing how people talk about others in negative ways. Metaphor in particular plays a powerful role in this mental picturing process. In 1915, for example, newspaper headlines designed to expel Armenians from the Ottoman Empire referred to the uprooting of "malignant weeds" in the land (Kuper 1981: 91). It is no coincidence that this type of speech preceded widespread violence against the Armenians and their mass displacement. Examples such as this abound in the annals of history. As Hobbs and Antonopoulos (2013: 44) have cogently argued, in the case of foreigners or immigrants, hate metaphors are often effective psychologically because they are connected to an inherent *alien conspiracy theory*, or the view that foreigners are responsible for endemic social ills. An example is the conspiratorial narrative used against Italian immigration to the US in the first decades of the twentieth century. The narrative revolved around the Black Hand extortion schemes of the era (Nicaso and Danesi 2020). These consisted of extortion letters sent to victims demanding money; each letter was signed with the picture of a black hand. The newspapers and the movies at the time portrayed such schemes as the result of opening up immigration from Italy to America. This portrayal created a negative picture in the mind, to use Lippmann's phrase, of all Italian immigrants as either part of crime families or as sympathetic to them. They were seen, in effect, as a "dangerous class," a term traced initially to a book by Honoré Antoine Frégier published in 1840, in which he links criminality to Italian character.

With the rise of populist and far-right political movements in the 2010s, the use of dehumanizing metaphors to engender hatred of foreigners or of those who are different in some way has spread worldwide. Among these animal and dirt metaphors are among the most common ones undergirding descriptions of outsiders or minorities as pests, reptiles, and parasites or as filthy or grimy. Poison metaphors also abound—in 2016, during a state-orchestrated public campaign against refugees and migrants in Hungary, the prime minister, Viktor Orbán, characterized them as a poison: "We don't need it and won't swallow it." Hate speech works psychologically because of the Korzybski effect, as it has been called here—it literally turns on the hate switch in some people, often incentivizing violent reactions. The hate-based speech of the white supremacist protestors during the violent unrest that took place in August 2017 in the city of Charlottesville, brought out how dehumanizing metaphors can and do lead to unrest and violence. These included hate slogans such as "Jews will not replace us" (an obvious antisemitic trope), "blood and soil" (a rendition of Nazi Germany's metaphorical *Blut und Boden*, to invoke patriotic nationalism), among others. The same type of speech was used in the January 6 insurrection on the American Capitol—ignited by Donald Trump's big lie and his constant use of slogans such as "save America" and "take it back" from democratic liberal élites. Korzybski (1921: 71) himself used the metaphor of poison to warn people of what such speech does to the brain:

> Humans can be literally poisoned by false ideas and false teachings. Many people have a just horror at the thought of putting poison into tea or coffee, but seem unable to realize that, when they teach false ideas and false doctrines, they are poisoning the time-binding capacity of their fellow men and women. One has to stop and think! There is nothing mystical about the fact that ideas and words are energies which powerfully affect the physico-chemical base of our time-binding activities. Humans are thus made untrue to "human nature." The conception of

man as a mixture of animal and supernatural has for ages kept human beings under the deadly spell of the suggestion that, animal selfishness and animal greediness are their essential character, and the spell has operated to suppress their real human nature and to prevent it from expressing itself naturally and freely.

Conspiracy Theories

Conspiracy theories are false narratives based on underlying metaphorical constructs, such as *immigrants are weeds* to be extricated from the native soil. These will be discussed in detail in Chapter 3. The goal here is to look at conspiracy theories in a general way. As Lewandowsky and Cook (2020: 3) remark, these are narratives that are not supported by any factual evidence, but nonetheless withstand scrutiny because they gain believability and durability through the logic of the narrative itself, which derives from underlying conceptualizations (metaphors). For example, the widespread belief that the 9/11 terrorist attacks were an "inside job" became a conspiracy theory shortly thereafter that continues to be believed by a broad spectrum of Americans. It thrives, perhaps, because of an inherent distrust in government in America (Hart and Graether 2018). Once this type of conspiratorial thinking becomes accepted as true then believers become "hyper-skeptical of all information that does not fit the theory, over-interpreting evidence that supports a preferred theory, and inconsistency" (Lewandowsky and Cook 2020: 3).

Among the reasons given by psychologists for the crystallization of conspiracy thinking is the feeling of powerlessness or vulnerability: "People who feel powerless or vulnerable are more likely to endorse and spread conspiracy theories, as can be seen in online forums where people's perceived level of threat is strongly linked to proposing conspiracy theories" (Lewandowsky and Cook 2020: 4). Such thinking is reinforced when small random events, such as intact windows in the Pentagon after the 9/11 attacks, are reinterpreted through the frame of the conspiracy theory— because if an airliner had really hit the Pentagon, then all windows would have shattered. This "connecting the dots" form of thinking is what gives conspiracies the logic of truth—a form of thinking called apophenia by psychologists, defined as the tendency to perceive connected meaning between unrelated events. It is this false logic that is exploited by groups, such as QAnon, who have emerged for no other reason than to promote conspiracies. Followers believe that an anonymous government insider, known as "Q," drops mysterious clues to expose the so-called "deep state" apparatus working behind the scenes against America and Americans. All one has to do to "see this" is connect the dots that Q sends to followers and the picture of what is behind the scenes will become clear. QAnon is an example of what happens to a society when a politically clever leader comes onto the scene to upset a society's emotional stability with systematic uses of lies and conspiracy stories, designed to stir up unconscious fears and bring them out in the open—that leader in America was Donald Trump. It is no coincidence that for QAnon followers Donald Trump was a secret agent fighting to save the world—a world populated by pedophiles and sex traffickers, led by Democratic politicians. As game designer Reed Berkowitz (2020) has remarked, QAnon followers may believe that they are involved in a kind of videogame with Trump as the victim who must be saved by connecting the clues left by Q; as he put it, QAnon is "gaming's evil twin, a game that plays people."

Conspiracies are similar to malicious gossip. As biologist Robin Dunbar (1997) has suggested, gossip reveals passive aggression, isolating and harming others, as it builds and maintains a sense of community among the gossipers. The same pattern unites conspiracy theory believers (Birchall 2006). Once the false message perpetrated by conspiracists has activated belief mechanisms, these cannot be turned off easily, since contrary facts are taken as evidence of its validity—a phenomenon called confirmation bias, the process of disregarding information that might disprove a belief while seeking information that supports it. This state of mind can be encapsulated as follows: "If so many believe it, then it must be true, especially since I myself can add something to the substance of the information." It is at such points of cognitive reflection that a conspiracy theory becomes impervious to falsification, as believers interpret any and all kinds of information as confirming it.

At this point a caveat is in order—one must always be wary of attacking those who espouse conspiracism. As David Harper (2008) has so aptly put it: "We should strive to be aware of what we are doing when labelling others as paranoid or reporting that they believe in conspiracy theories, given that one of the effects of such a move is to undermine the legitimacy of others' views and to implicitly position our own views as legitimate." All the analyst can (and should) do is to deconstruct the linguistic forms that undergird conspiracy thinking, and present them for discussion and debate both within the science of linguistics and within the larger society.

Metaphor and Deception

The objective of metaphor study within cognitive linguistics is to understand how the human brain extracts elements from disparate information, organizing them into meaningful wholes (Turner and Fauconnier 1995, 1997, Fauconnier and Turner 2000). Why do we interpret a sentence such as "That politician is a snake" not in literal terms but as a dangerous individual, given that politicians and snakes belong to different species? That is the central question posed within cognitive linguistics—as will be discussed throughout the remainder of this book.

The point of departure for studying metaphor systematically within linguistics can be traced to 1977, when a team of psychologists, headed by Howard Pollio, published a watershed investigation which found that everyday conversations are structured by metaphorical thinking. Titled *Psychology and the Poetics of Growth: Figurative Language in Psychology, Psychotherapy, and Education*, the researchers found that speakers of English uttered, on average, 3,000 novel metaphors and 7,000 idioms (frozen metaphors) per week on average (Pollio et al. 1977). This was followed by the 1979 collection of studies edited by Andrew Ortony, *Metaphor, and*

Thought, the 1980 anthology put together by Richard P. Honeck and Robert R. Hoffman, *Cognition and Figurative Language*, and the 1980 book by George Lakoff and Mark Johnson, *Metaphors We Live By*, which, together, set the groundwork for cognitive linguistics to become established as a school of linguistics putting forth a specific type of semantic-conceptual analysis. The central notion on which it is implanted is that metaphorical meaning pervades language and thought. If contextual information is missing from an utterance such as "The murderer is an animal," our inclination is to interpret it metaphorically, not literally. It is only if we are told that the *murderer* is an actual nonhuman animal (a bear, a cougar, etc.) that a literal interpretation comes into focus. And even then, by calling a bear a murderer we are attributing human characteristics to it, since murder is an intentional human act of killing. As Lakoff (1979) aptly put it: "metaphor is a major and indispensable part of our ordinary, conventional way of conceptualizing the world, and that our everyday behavior reflects our metaphorical understanding of experience." This does not deny the presence of literal meaning—as he goes on to observe: "a sentence like 'The balloon went up' is not metaphorical, nor is the old philosopher's favorite 'The cat is on the mat.' But as soon as one gets away from the concrete physical experience and starts talking about abstractions or emotions, metaphorical understanding is the norm" (Lakoff 1979). Lakoff went on to establish *conceptual metaphor theory* as a framework for investigating abstract meaning-making as grounded in metaphorical cognition.

Conceptual metaphor theory will be discussed in the next chapter. Here it is sufficient to point out that if its claims are valid, even in a minimal way, then the reason why metaphor can be used as a powerful tool for deception, not just as a means for grasping abstractions, comes into focus—a view that was held by various philosophers prior to cognitive linguistics. For example, in his classic book, *Essay Concerning Humane Understanding*, philosopher John Locke pinpointed metaphor as the source for deception, advising that it be avoided in the search for truth and knowledge (Locke 1690: 34):

> If we would speak of things as they are, we must allow that all the art of rhetoric, besides order and clearness, all the artificial and figurative application of words eloquence hath invented, are for nothing else but to insinuate wrong ideas, move the passions, and thereby mislead the judgment; and so indeed are perfect cheats: and therefore, however laudable or allowable oratory may render them in harangues and popular addresses, they are certainly, in all discourses that pretend to inform or instruct, wholly to be avoided; and where truth and knowledge are concerned, cannot but be thought a great fault, either of language or person that makes use of them.

Even before Locke, Thomas Hobbes (1651, 1656) characterized metaphor as an obstacle to communication, a source of ambiguity and deceit, and thus, a feature of speech to be eliminated from philosophical and scientific investigations. Hobbes was particularly perturbed by its use by political orators to deceive people (Tralau 2014), arguing that metaphor stimulates an "aesthetic pleasure" within us that dupes us into accepting it as meaningful. As Feldman (2001: 21) notes, "Hobbes saw the most dangerous metaphor [as the one] that corrupts knowledge and thereby makes error and deception possible." It leads to a corruption of conscience, since it distorts the truth. Whatever one may think of Hobbes's overall philosophy, clearly his description of the deceptive power of metaphor was an apt one, since he saw it as the basis for the persuasive effects of politically motivated lies.

The same perspective was elaborated later by Friedrich Nietzsche in his 1873 essay, *On Truth and Lies in a Nonmoral Sense*. Nietzsche came to see metaphor as humanity's greatest flaw, because of its unconscious power to persuade people into believing it on its own terms—and that is why, he asserted, it is the source of the most callous of lies, especially because it is "invisible." Nietzsche divided human thought into two domains—the domain of perception, consisting of impressions and sensations, and the domain of conception, consisting of the ideas that the mind infers from perception. But conception, Nietzsche asserted, is not a straightforward inferential process, but rather, the result of linking impressions together. This linkage is imprinted in the structure of metaphor which, subsequently, has the effect of distorting the true perception of things, creating belief because it prods the mind into perceiving a resemblance among disparate things by simply linking them together in linguistic form. Metaphor is thus the source of our false belief systems. In effect, Nietzsche saw metaphor as a linguistic self-fulfilling prophecy.

Coming long before the cognitive linguistic movement, Nietzsche's assessment, as pessimistic as it is, envisioned metaphor as a mind-forming and mind-altering mode of discourse. Nietzsche even realized that the nefarious liar can use it to turn falsehoods into truths in people's minds (Nietzsche 1879):

> The liar is a person who uses the valid designations, the words, in order to make something which is unreal appear to be real. He says, for example, "I am rich," when the proper designation for his condition would be "poor." He misuses fixed conventions by means of arbitrary substitutions or even reversals of names. If he does this in a selfish and moreover harmful manner, society will cease to trust him and will thereby exclude him. What men avoid by excluding the liar is not so much being defrauded as it is being harmed by means of fraud. Thus, even at this stage, what they hate is basically not deception itself, but rather the unpleasant, hated consequences of certain sorts of deception. It is in a similarly restricted sense that man now wants nothing but truth: he desires the pleasant, life-preserving consequences of truth. He is indifferent toward pure knowledge which has no consequences.

Nietzsche went on to ask the following key question: "What is a word?" Prefiguring Korzybski, his own answer is revelatory: "It is the copy in sound of a nerve stimulus. But the further inference from the nerve stimulus to a cause outside of us is already the result of a false and unjustifiable application of the principle of sufficient reason" (Nietzsche 1879). It is in fact the application that makes metaphor powerful. Recall the snake metaphor above; Nietzsche discussed this exact same metaphor as follows: "We speak of a snake: this designation touches only upon its ability to twist itself and could therefore also fit a worm. What arbitrary differentiations! What one-sided preferences, first for this, then for that property of a thing!" As Mark Turner (1997) has commented, metaphor does indeed seem to have a kind of mental metamorphosis effect, whereby we can see a person turning into a snake in our imagination, experiencing the metamorphosis psychosomatically. Franz Kafka played on this power of metaphor in his 1915 novella *Die Verwandlung* ("The Metamorphosis"), which starts with a salesman waking one morning to find himself transformed into a monstrous vermin. Kafka's tale constitutes a disorienting assault on literal meaning, but in so doing it impels us to search for a hidden meaning. Metaphor works in this way—hence its power to shape minds, for the better or worse. In sum, for Nietzsche thought is "a movable host of metaphors, metonymies, and anthropomorphisms: in short, a sum of human relations which have been poetically and rhetorically intensified, transferred, and embellished, and which, after long usage, seem to a people to be fixed, canonical, and binding" (Nietzsche 1879).

What makes metaphor powerful, as Nietzsche understood (perhaps for the first time) is that it is unconscious, and thus more likely to permanently affect how we perceive something. And what makes it more effective is that it leaves permanent semantic residues in the conceptual system of a language, in the form of frozen metaphors, which thus work latently on thought systems. Take, for example, the metaphor of war in politics, which Lakoff and Johnson (1980) see as a potent shaper of thought, used to create or support political ideologies, forge beliefs, shape attitudes, and the like. This is an ancient military metaphor. An example of its use can be found in *The Meditations* of Roman emperor Marcus Aurelius as can be seen in the following two excerpts (in Robertson 2021):

Life is warfare, and a sojourn in foreign land.

Be not ashamed to be helped for it is your business to do your duty like a soldier in the assault on a town. How then, if being lame you cannot mount up on the battlements alone, but with the help of another it is possible?

As Lakoff and Johnson observe, the war metaphor, as a latent form of thought, implies that political "battles" can be "won" or "lost," policy positions can be "attacked" or "guarded," progress can be "gained" or "lost," lines of "attack" can be "abandoned" or "defended," and so on. These warlike images are so embedded in our minds that we do not normally realize that they guide our perception of, and emotional reactions to, arguments, ideas, and speeches in politics. Expressions such as a "battle of ideas" or the election was "fought on a dangerous battleground" evoke an image of bellicosity which likely produces a Korzybski effect. From this central metaphor, we derive offshoots, such as politicians are "soldiers," fighting for one side or the other, with different "strategies" and "tactics," and so on.

It is truly remarkable that we are so susceptible to metaphorical language, as Nietzsche warned. The war metaphor is so embedded in our unconscious mind that it can be seen to guide or influence behavior, ideology, and the like. Metaphors not only communicate ideas but also shape them. In immigration policy, for example, America once described itself as a "melting pot," with people from many cultures blending into its social fabric; but the "war on immigration," exacerbated by the Trump administration in the US stands in jarring contrast to the melting pot image. Politics is often a "battle" of contrasting metaphorical images. When President Jimmy Carter declared "the moral equivalent of war" on energy consumption, he transformed the challenge into a matter of national security, calling for wartime sacrifices. However, a primary problem with such war metaphors is that they engender and instill an actual sense of conflict, as can be seen today in the divisive politics in countries across the world.

Aristotle (2009) held that virtues such as justice, charity, and generosity benefitted both the person possessing them and society generally, implying logically that these are necessary antidotes to the destructive effects of lies and deceit. Since antiquity, humans have held up ethical behavior as our main protection against mendacity and deceit—that is, as the only way to counteract the manipulative power of the masterful liar. Cognitive linguistics is not a solution to this state of affairs; all it can do is to decode the kind of language utilized by the liar, which Locke, Hobbes, and Nietzsche insightfully saw as the most destructive of human social harmony.

Epilogue

Lying manifests itself in a host of verbal behaviors, from simple fibbing to deceit and dissimulation. Understanding what lying is, in an age of political conspiracies and social media falsehoods is critical. The master liar can fabricate falsehoods on the spot for opportunistic reasons, veiling them as truths ingeniously. Immanuel Kant (1790), like Augustine before him, argued that all persons are born with intrinsic dignity, capable of freely making their own decisions, setting their own goals, and guiding their behavior by reason. To be human, said Kant, is to have the power of free choice; to be ethical, he continued, is to respect that power in others. Lies are morally wrong, therefore, for two reasons—they impede the ability to make free, rational choices, interfering with people's habitual thinking processes based on ethical behavior, and they manipulate hidden feelings by putting them into words.

The Dreyfus Affair showed that lies that become politicized will sow division, stoking prejudices and fears. The same effect was caused by Donald Trump's big lie that the 2020 election was stolen from him by nefarious actors behind the scenes. The parallels between the two cases are remarkable. Evidence showed from the outset that Esterhazy's claim was a big lie, triggering political divisiveness; evidence of fraudulent vote-counting methods analogously showed that Trump's claim was a big lie as well, similarly triggering divisiveness in America. In France, the French Army was the entity that advanced the big lie at first, but it soon after broadened out to a whole constellation of right-wing political actors; in the Trump case, at first it was he himself, aided by unscrupulous lawyers and politicians, who advanced the big lie, but it too quickly broadened out to encompass a substantial sector of the Republican Party. Clearly, politically motivated lies tend to produce the same kind of effects, regardless of era or political actors involved.

Once a big lie spreads, the forces of division deepen, gradually becoming fossilized. The other side is seen more and more not as wrong but wicked. Politics becomes a winner-takes-all proposition. And the threat of political violence that resided below the surface becomes ominous and real. A big lie must, however, be implanted on a metaphorical cognitive substratum to work effectively—as will be argued in this book. Symbols, emblems, and other nonverbal structures that are associated with a political cause are derivatives of the underlying metaphor, which often harkens back to ancient images. British politician Enoch Powell's divisive "rivers of blood" speech, for example, linked immigration policy to the ominous prophecy in Virgil's *Aeneid* where the river Tiber is described as "foaming with much blood;" the American president Franklin D. Roosevelt used the war metaphor in his inauguration speech, when he proclaimed: "I assume unhesitatingly the leadership of this great army of our people dedicated to a disciplined attack upon our common problems," which allowed workers in post-depression America to imagine themselves as soldiers in a battle. As Aristotle claimed in his *Rhetoric* (see 1952), the ability to forge a conceptual linkage between two things, such as a workforce and an army, generates powerful meaning, since it can collapse complex problems into simple linguistic forms, making them intelligible and cogent in an intuitive way.

Hitler rose to power because of a massive big lie of a Jewish cabal operating behind the scenes and aiming to gain control of the world—Hitler actually accused the Jews of being the liars, thus using a form of projection whereby his victim (the Jews) became the victimizer. It was one of Germany's military leaders, Erich Ludendorff, who had proclaimed publicly that Jewish people had been responsible for Germany's World War I defeat. In 1922 he wrote (cited in Cohn 1967: 149): "The supreme government of the Jewish people was working hand in hand with France and England. Perhaps it was leading them both." As proof, he offered what turned out to be a conspiracy theory—namely, a document called the *Protocols of the Elders of Zion*, which supposedly contained the notes taken at a secret meeting of Jewish leaders to allegedly take over the world. The *Protocols* was a forgery, written by the Russian secret police in the early 1900s to incite hatred against Jewish peoples. Nonetheless, many believed that the *Protocols* explained seemingly "inexplicable" events, such as the war, the economic crises that followed the war, the revolutions in Russia, and even pandemics. That conspiracy is still believed to this day, indicating how difficult it is to eradicate a big lie when it is perpetrated.

Significantly, it catapulted Hitler to power, who utilized the lie to suppress political opponents and the free media, labeling them as "enemies of the people," a phrase that originated in Roman times and used for centuries subsequently, given new life by Stalin during his despotic reign and then by Donald Trump to attack news organizations and journalists whom he perceived as biased against him.

The following points synthesize the discussion in this chapter.

1 Deconstructing the metaphors used in the construction of big lies and conspiracy theories will normally reveal underlying ideological motives. So, when a political actor describes a certain group as "weeds" to be extricated from a nation, the metaphor can be seen to tap into the idyllic view of a nation as a garden with natural plants that will be destroyed by weeds unless they are eliminated.
2 Big lies do not portray events as due to happenstance, but rather as having been orchestrated. False evidence is used to support them.
3 Lies and conspiracy theories shape beliefs, often igniting or reigniting divisions in society.
4 Conspiracy theories claim to uncover how events are linked, ascribing them to imaginary secret cabals who are constantly plotting against world order.
5 Believers tend to interpret any contrary evidence as confirming it. When a disagreement between those who believe a lie and those who do not becomes extreme, the rift between the two sides hardens.
6 The links that conspiracy theories create are the threads that hold the narrative together conceptually; if any of these is disconnected the whole narrative might fall apart.

Alfred Dreyfus himself issued a warning about big lies and their harmful effects on democracies, which is worth repeating here as a final word (in Dreyfus 1937: 175): "If you shut up truth and bury it under the ground, it will but grow, and gather to itself such explosive power that the day it bursts through it will blow up everything in its way."

2

DECONSTRUCTING POLITICAL LIES

Prologue

The use of metaphor in political speeches is, arguably, what makes them so effective and memorable—for good or bad. A classic example of the former is Martin Luther King's *I Have a Dream* speech, which he delivered in Washington, DC on August 28, 1963, during the March on Washington for Jobs and Freedom. The speech connects the plight of African Americans to the American Dream, which had never been a possibility for many. Evoking religious imagery via metaphor, King, who was a Baptist minister, implored his fellow citizens as follows: "Let us not wallow in the valley of despair. I say to you today, my friends, so even though we face the difficulties of today and tomorrow, I still have a dream. It is a dream deeply rooted in the American dream" (in King 2022). The metaphor of the valley of despair resonated profoundly with many at the time (and still does), given that it evoked images of dispossessed people especially in the Bible, such as the ancient Hebrews, who sought a way out of their despair by searching for the "promised land."

Among other key metaphors that King used to make his speech forceful, the following stand out:

- *Banking notes:* "It is obvious today that America has defaulted on this promissory note insofar as her citizens of color are concerned," which encapsulates the fact that America had not come through in giving African Americans the same freedoms and privileges of white Americans.
- *Drinking cups:* "Let us not seek to satisfy our thirst for freedom by drinking from the cup of bitterness and hatred," which evokes religious images of dinking from cups and chalices throughout the Old and New Testaments.

DOI: 10.4324/9781003349143-2

- *Doors*: "Now is the time to open the doors of opportunity to all of God's children." This metaphor reaches back considerably in time to the image of mythic portals as thresholds to new worlds of justice, which King reinforces subsequently as follows: "But there is something that I must say to my people who stand on the warm threshold which leads into the palace of justice."
- *Nature*: "Now is the time to lift our nation from the quick sands of racial injustice to the solid rock of brotherhood;" "No, no, we are not satisfied, and we will not be satisfied until justice rolls down like waters and righteousness like a mighty stream." These metaphors project the imagination into natural settings which encapsulate the plight of African Americans as entrapped in social "quick sands," from which they must be "lifted" and put on a "solid rock of brotherhood." The mental transmutation that these images induce allows us to concretely grasp the "racial injustice" present in America.
- *Music*: "With this faith we will be able to transform the jangling discords of our nation into a beautiful symphony of brotherhood." This evokes a powerful synesthetic effect—an aural change from cacophonic dissonance ("jangling discords") to one of racial consonance ("A beautiful symphony").

There is little doubt that the speech was instrumental in sparking a society-wide movement towards racial equality, which is still ongoing. In cognitive linguistics, King's expressions are called more precisely *source domains*, which are concrete concepts (referring to nature, music, and so on) mapped onto the overall abstract *target domain* of the speech—racial justice. Now, while in this case the metaphorical mapping is used for a positive cause, the very same mechanism is used to make political lies persuasive. While there are other rhetorical strategies used in persuasion, certainly the use of metaphor is a primary one. This chapter will focus on metaphor, providing a schematic overview of conceptual metaphor theory, which, as mentioned (Chapter 1), was developed largely at first by George Lakoff, who like Nietzsche, understood its value to decoding politics as based on powerful metaphorical discourse.

It is relevant to note that Lakoff, and others who use conceptual metaphor theory in political analysis, are often labeled "left-wing," reproached for using their knowledge as a tool against conservative ideology, which would make the applications of the theory non-objective. But this critique is not justified. While any theory can be used for self-serving political motives, by and large, conceptual metaphor theory has been applied to any and all types of political speeches, from the left or the right. Lakoff has used the theory in fact to deconstruct the political rhetoric used by liberals and conservatives alike. His overall aim has been to show what is psychologically behind "words that work." In his 1987 book, *Women, Fire, and Dangerous Things*, Lakoff answered the critiques by using an evidence-based approach to language, showing that it is independent of any political ideology. In further response to the criticisms, Lakoff and Rafael E. Núñez showed how conceptual metaphor theory could be used in any area of human understanding, such as mathematics, beyond any intimation of political bias (Lakoff and Núñez 2000).

Conceptual Metaphors

Consider again the expression discussed in the previous chapter: "That politician is a snake." This is hardly just a figure of speech, meant to replace literal language for emphasis. It brings out that we perceive human character in a metaphorical way. As such, it is only one manifestation of an unconscious thought formula, *people are animals*, known as a *conceptual metaphor*. In it, the *people* part is called the *target* domain, as mentioned above, and the *animal* part is called the *source* domain. The different expressions that this formula undergirds are the actual *linguistic metaphors* that are used in everyday speech:

> That official is a puppy.
> Our counselor is a butterfly.
> Your opponent is a tiger.
> That politician is a pussycat.
> That politician, instead, is a gorilla.

Conceptual metaphors are the result of mapping source domains onto target domains. In the case above, the source domain (*animals*) provides the lexical resources (*puppy, butterfly, tiger,* etc.) that are mapped onto the target domain of *people* (politicians, friends, enemies, etc.). The mapping is unconscious and systematic. Each linguistic metaphor produced is thus a mini-psychological profile of different human personalities in terms of perceived nonhuman animal characteristics, akin to a miniature poem.

Before cognitive linguistics, the study of metaphor fell within the field of rhetoric, where it was viewed as a specific type of trope. But since Lakoff and Johnson's 1980 book, the practice has been to use the term *metaphor* to refer to the study of mappings of all kinds. Within this framework *personification*, for instance ("My cat speaks Italian"), would be seen as a particular kind of mapping, one in which the target domain is an *animal* and the source domain *human characteristics*, which is a reversal of the *people are animals* conceptual metaphor. However, as Lakoff and Johnson (1980) argued, there are two tropes that should be considered separately from metaphor—metonymy and irony. Metonymy is the process by which the name of one thing is used in place of another associated with or suggested by it (the *White House* for *the American government*). In conceptual terms, it can also be defined as a mapping—in this case, a part of a domain (the *White House*) is mapped onto the whole domain (the *American government*) (Lakoff and Johnson 1980: 35–40). So, while metonymy is ontologically different from metaphor, it still reveals that mapping is involved as a conceptual mechanism, and thus need not be differentiated for practical purposes, including those pertinent to this book. For example, the use of the face as a metonym for personality involves the mapping structure, *the face is the person,* which manifests itself commonly in expressions such as the following:

He's just another pretty face.
There are an awful lot of faces in the audience.
We need some new faces around here.
You can read his thoughts on his face.

Irony is the use of words to convey a meaning contrary to their literal sense. This too can be envisioned as a mapping—namely the projection of a source domain that contains antonymic meaning structures onto the target domain—that is, ironic concepts are formed by mapping source domains (*torture, torment,* etc.) incongruously onto target domains (*love, enjoyment,* etc.):

You love being tortured, don't you?
Your friend loves getting hurt.
Your cousin enjoys torment.

Historically, metaphor has always been considered a powerful form of oratory, starting with Aristotle, who discovered it and named it as such. The Roman orator Cicero can be seen even to provide the first implicit definition of a conceptual metaphor (in Cicero 1942: 274):

All metaphors, at least such of them that are best chosen, are applied to the senses, especially the seeing, which of all senses is the most exquisite. Thus when we say, the tincture of politeness, the softness of good-breeding, the murmur of waters, and sweetness of language; these metaphors are all taken from the other senses. But the metaphors taken from the sense of seeing are much more striking, because they place in the eye of the imagination of objects otherwise impossible for us to see or comprehend. For there is nothing in nature but what we may adapt its name to signify something else; and every object from which a likeness may be raised, as it may from all objects, if metaphorically applied.

Cicero's "tincture," "softness," "murmur," and "sweetness" figures of speech are precursors of the notion of source domain and of the related notion of *image schema* (Lakoff 1987, Johnson 1987, Lakoff and Johnson 1999). The latter is a mental percept that guides the selection of particular source domains as relevant in the mapping process. Image schemas are mental extrapolations of physical experiences or sensations such as those connected with orientation—*up*-versus-*down*, *back*-versus-*front*, *near*-versus-*far*, etc. These then guide the formation of various abstract concepts such as *happiness* ("Lately my spirits are up"), *responsibility* ("You have to face up to your problems"), *life* ("You have a long life ahead of you"), *love* ("They are very close to each other"), among many others. As another example, consider the common experience of how containers work and what they allow us to do, which is extrapolated by the brain and turned into an image schema that then guides the understanding of concepts such as *mind* ("My mind is full of good memories"), *emotions* ("My heart is filled with hope"), and so on. This is known, logically, as the *container* schema.

In the Martin Luther King speech above, the image schemas guiding his selection of source domains can be broken down as follows:

Image Schema	Metaphorical Concept
promissory note	America has defaulted on its promissory note to African Americans
cups	We must no longer drink from a cup of hatred
doors	Previously closed doors must be opened up to all Americans
natural forms	We all belong to Nature equally
bells	Bells ring out to both unite people spiritually and to warn them of the need for action

One image schema that requires special commentary is that of the *journey,* since it is intrinsic to the entire speech: "And they have come to realize that their freedom is inextricably bound to our freedom. We cannot walk alone. And as we walk, we must make the pledge that we shall always march ahead. We cannot turn back." In journeys, one might come across obstacles or impediments that come in the way of the journey towards freedom. The implication is that removing these can only be achieved by always "marching ahead."

Metaphorical Framing

King employed source domains suggested by different image schemas to frame his pleas for racial justice. Here are a few other excerpts exemplifying how King framed his entreaties:

Utterance: "One hundred years later, the Negro lives on a lonely island of poverty in the midst of a vast ocean of material prosperity. One hundred years later the Negro is still languished in the corners of American society and finds himself in exile in his own land."

Source domains: islands, ocean, exile

Target domain: racial isolation

Frame: Islands emphasize isolation for those in social exile in the midst of a vast ocean. By framing the plight of African Americans in this way, King is inviting a deeper examination of the hopelessness of racial isolation.

Utterance: "Now is the time to rise from the dark and desolate valley of segregation to the sunlit path of racial justice."

Source domains: valley, darkness, path

Target domain: racial justice

Frame: Valleys are lower places that leave people desolate in darkness and desolation (a form of emotional isolation). The path image schema is a powerful one for representing the search for racial justice, which will eliminate the darkness and bring about sunlight.

Utterance: "Now is the time to lift our nation from the quicksands of racial injustice to the solid rock of brotherhood."

Source domains: quicksands, rocks

Target domain: racial harmony and unity

Frame: Quicksand refers to loose wet sand that pulls in anything resting on or falling into it, thus alluding to the emotional and social quagmire in which African Americans find themselves, from which it is hard to escape. To be able to do so requires a "lifting up" and relocation on a "solid rock of brotherhood."

Utterance: "I have a dream that one day every valley shall be exalted, every hill and mountain shall be made low, the rough places will be made plain, and the crooked places will be made straight."

Source domains: hills and mountains, roughness, crookedness

Target domain: equality of the races

Frame: Equality will be achieved after the hills and mountains that African Americans face will be "made low" and their rough and crooked formations will be made "plain" (smooth) and "straight" (correct).

Lakoff (2004) defined metaphorical framing as the use of conceptual metaphors to influence people's decision-making by mapping common experiences onto abstractions (recalling Cicero), giving them an easier-to-comprehend form. The notion is traced to the work of Michael Reddy (1979), who argued that some conceptual metaphors are based on universal image schemas, while others are more culture-specific. Two universal ones are the *conduit* and *container* image schemas, whereby mental states (feelings, ideas, concepts, etc.) are perceived to be substances that are put into linguistic containers (words, sentences, etc.), whose meanings are then extracted by listeners or readers, akin to taking substances or objects out of their containers, and then passed on to others (as in a conduit). The notion of "thought," which is a vague one, can only be understood through such frames, which portray it as existing in a "space" containing ideas into which people can enter to insert or take away ideas (Reddy 1979: 291–292). Frames also guide subsequent metaphorizing—a cognitive phenomenon that Lakoff (1979: 223) called *invariance*; namely the fact that metaphors preserve the image-schema structure of the initial source domain, in a way that is consistent with the inherent structure of the target domain: "source domain interiors correspond to target domain interiors; source domain exteriors correspond to target domain exteriors; etc. … One cannot find cases where a source domain interior is mapped onto a target domain exterior, or where a source domain exterior is mapped onto a target domain path. This simply does not happen."

So, by framing the need for social justice as a path towards a goal (as did King above), the image schema of movement crops up in the mind which then motivates action. As neuroscientific research has found (Feldman and Narayan 2004) the likely reason for this is that the part in the brain that encodes the concept of justice and another that encodes the experience of paths are activated together forming a circuit that combines both concepts. Research by Boulenger, Shtyrov, and Pulvermuller (2012) also found that metaphors depicting a physical activity, such as the path (journey) one, are processed in the brain's motor cortex much faster than literal language, influencing the extent to which people pay attention to ideas framed metaphorically.

King intuitively knew, as a Baptist minister, that framing social justice issues with images such as valleys, mountains, paths, and so on was persuasive because they were deeply embedded in religious and social justice writings and would thus reverberate with his overall theme of achieving the "dream" of equality. Metaphorical framing is different than other framing methods (Gentner and Jeziorski 1993). In analogies, for example, the source and the target domains must be similar—not so in metaphorical framing. The classic example is the analogy of the structure of the solar system to the structure of an atom, where a similarity of structures is assumed. In a metaphor, on the other hand, the similarity is not assumed beforehand; it is created by the mapping. No child assumes a similarity between a person and a snake until a metaphor is used to connect them. At that point, a similarity comes into focus by itself. Metaphorical framing is also different from so-called episodic and thematic framing (Aarøe 2011), which emphasizes the scope of a problem, that is, whether it is looked at through a personal lens (episodic) or in general terms (thematic). Again, metaphorical framing produces the scope itself, as can be seen in King's framing of social justice issues. This very same strategy is used to frame stereotypical discourses. For instance, by framing immigration as a flood (for example, "a wave of refugees") the problem comes into mental focus in a concrete way, and the frame can thus be used to support a wall at a border crossing, as Trump constantly declared during his presidency (Jimenez, Arndt, and Landau 2021). Analyzing social media posts during the presidency, the researchers above found that people who supported building a wall to prevent immigrants from coming into the United States were more likely to frame immigration as a flood than people who did not support the wall. The flood frame clearly activated in people's minds associations of flood-prevention strategies, including the building of walls.

Politically Motivated Lies

It is in the domain of politically motivated lying that conceptual metaphor theory can be used fruitfully to deconstruct the conceptual sources of lies and conspiratorial narratives so as to understand how they gain their persuasive power. Political manipulators use the same type of frames as those discussed above, but twist them for self-serving purposes. King's ultimate goal was the attainment of social justice for African Americans, but the political manipulator's ultimate goal is self-enhancement, self-perpetuation, and Orwellian mind control.

The consummate liar knows (intuitively) how to use metaphorical frames for political or financial gain, able to fabricate falsehoods for opportunistic reasons, veiling them as truths. The politically-motivated liar is a master wordsmith, who is able to wreak moral chaos on the polity through his deceitful use of metaphorically-based discourse frames designed to create a mind fog that obscures reality and produces its own illusory world. He does this through constant mind-numbing repetition of the same frames in the form of slogans and catchwords. As Ruth Ben-Ghiat (2106) has argued, this type of strategy has always been adopted by despots. Italian dictator Benito Mussolini, for example, confounded everyone when he came onto the political scene with his earthy language, setting himself apart from the intelligentsia of his era, tapping into people's sense that the intellectuals looked down on everyone who did not think like them. He founded an "anti-party" just after World War I, recalling Orwellian doublespeak. He presented himself as a disrupter of the status quo, challenging the traditional politics of the nation, promising to restore Italy to its great past: "A nation of spaghetti eaters cannot restore Roman civilization (cited in Mussolini 2018)." The image of spaghetti-eaters as an image schema clearly was one of his strategic discourse frames that in hindsight obviously worked emotionally on his followers, who catapulted him to power.

Among the many metaphorical frames used by Mussolini, the following can be mentioned as cases-in-point (cited in Mussolini 2020):

Utterance: "The country is young, but its institutions are old; and when a conflict between new forces and old institutions begins to shape itself, that means that the new wine cannot any longer be kept in the old skins, or the inevitable will occur. The old forces of the political and social life of Italy will fall into fragments."

Source domains: youth, wine, fragments

Target domain: existing social institutions

Frame: Mussolini uses the metaphor of youth as an allusion to renewal, rebirth, and thus a force for change, which like wine (a powerful nationalistic metaphorical construct) will become stale if kept in its "old skins." With young people at the forefront, the older institutions will fall into fragments. Fragmentation is also a powerful metaphor, given that polities are typically metaphorized as "bodies" (as in the "body politic"), as Rainer Guldin (2002) has observed: "The body and its parts have come to be viewed as text, trope, or metaphor, allowing one to think of the social systems." With this frame, Mussolini is promising to restore the wholeness to the body politic.

Utterance: "We Socialists who were in favour of intervention advocated war, because we divined that it contained within it the seeds of revolution. It is not the first instance of revolutionary war. There were the Napoleonic wars, the war of 1870, the enterprises of Garibaldi, in which, had we lived in those days, we should have joined in the same spirit and same faith."

Source domains: seeds, spirit, faith

Target domain: overthrow of the political status quo

Frame: Here, Mussolini frames the supposed need to change Italy in terms of the planting of "seeds of revolution." This rural metaphor fits in ontologically with Italy's history and, by implication, how the country is a fertile field that can be re-planted with new seeds to recreate the aims of Garibaldi, the legendary hero of Italian Unification in the nineteenth century, whose forces captured Sicily away from the Bourbon occupiers in 1861, thus playing a key role in the establishment of Italy as a united kingdom.

Utterance: "Our destiny cannot become universal unless it is transplanted to the pagan ground of Rome. By means of paganism Rome found her form and found the means of upholding herself in the world."

Source domains: religion, supporting structure

Target domain: Italian history

Frame: In this utterance, Mussolini uses the source domain of religion as the founding principle of Roman society, implying that Italy needs to do something similar, so that it can be restructured in a morally upright (upholding) position. One can easily imagine through this frame the ancient Roman statues of gods and goddesses as symbols of Rome's purported divine nature—a society and race chosen by the divinities, recalling Hitler's similar use of divine mythology (to be discussed subsequently).

Mussolini's utterances are grounded on politically manipulative metaphorical frames, including intertextual ones, which is a common strategy of persuasive political oratory. Recall Martin Luther King's allusions to biblical images and to themes of persecution. These resonated deeply with African Americans, because they alluded to religious texts with which they would have been familiar. Mussolini also used intertextuality effectively, albeit for a manipulative reason, as can be seen in his allusions to Garibaldi and to Roman paganism, which were textualized in historically pertinent books. Such intertextual mappings reinforce beliefs and expectations, since they allude to canonical texts that have special value to the group.

The notion of intertextuality was introduced by semiotician Julia Kristeva (1969) and elaborated later by Roland Barthes (1981). As Barthes pointed out, a text of any kind is constituted by bits of keywords, conventional formulas, and allusions to other texts, all of which pass into the text and are reconfigured within it. For Kristeva a text is the result of transforming other texts. Metaphor makes the transformation possible by enlisting the other texts as source domains that are mapped onto whatever target domain is relevant in a specific location within the text. To outsiders, this may appear to be meaningless, but to insiders, it is part of the creation of a coherent unity of meaning embedded in the discourse frame that evokes powerful emotions. Such texts keep people bound to each other unconsciously (Lévi-Strauss 1962).

A master of political metaphor as a means to bind people together was Vladimir Lenin, the founder of Soviet Communism in 1917. Below are relevant excerpts from a speech given by Lenin at an international meeting in Berne, on February 8, 1916, which he framed on the basis of a war source domain that he mapped onto different target domains to maximum effect; the speech was given just before the official end of World War I on June 28, 1919 (cited in Lenin 2011):

> *Excerpt:* "It may sound incredible, especially to Swiss comrades, but it is nevertheless true that in Russia, also, not only bloody tsarism, not only the capitalists, but also a section of the so-called ex-Socialists say that Russia is fighting a "war of defense," that Russia is only fighting against German invasion."
>
> *Source domains:* blood, war
>
> *Target domain:* Russian nationalism
>
> *Frame:* Lenin alludes indirectly to blood as a symbol of the new Russia, which is moving away from "bloody tsarism." The war metaphor is framed as one of defense, which is a clever metaphorical switch, since in this case the war is an action used defensively to resist attacks against the nation.
>
> *Excerpt:* "All the Great Powers are waging an imperialist, capitalist war, a predatory war, a war for the oppression of small and foreign nations, a war for the sake of the profits of the capitalists, who are coining golden profits amounting to billions out of the appalling sufferings of the masses, out of the blood of the proletariat."
>
> *Source domains:* predation, war, blood
>
> *Target domain:* capitalism
>
> *Frame:* Lenin uses the notion of predation as a frame for conveying how capitalism is a ruthless predator that wages a "capitalist war" that ultimately brings about the spilling of the "blood of the proletariat," measured in profits.
>
> *Excerpt:* "The millions of victims who will fall in the war, and as a consequence of the war, will not fall in vain. The millions who are starving, the millions who

are sacrificing their lives in the trenches, are not only suffering, they are also gathering strength, are pondering over the real cause of the war, are becoming more determined and are acquiring a clearer revolutionary understanding. Rising discontent of the masses, growing ferment, strikes, demonstrations, protests against the war—all this is taking place in all countries of the world. And this is the guarantee that the European War will be followed by the proletarian revolution against capitalism."

Source domains: war, upwards orientation

Target: capitalism

Frame: Lenin assails capitalism by mapping war images (victims, falling to war, trenches) onto the supposed plight of people in capitalist societies whose discontent is "rising" (orientation metaphor), leading, as in revolutions of the past, to a war against the system that supports capitalism.

Lenin's use of the war metaphor just before a real devastating war was about to end was a clever framing strategy, whereby a disastrous situation that he attributes to imperialist capitalism is contrasted against the positivity of the political uprising and revolution that had occurred in Russia at the time. The war of defense notion is tied conceptually to blood, which is shed to defend the proletariat, and which binds people together. Lenin's subtext is that Soviet Russia faced a threat from the outside, and thus, by implication that it required a "war of defense" enacted against those who would interfere with its political-social system.

The exact same subtext was built by Vladimir Putin into his speech to justify his invasion of Ukraine on February 24, 2020, blaming NATO as the motivation for his actions: "The war machine is moving and, I repeat, it is coming close to our borders" (cited in Putin 2020). The image of military machinery moving near to Russia is a projection mapping, whereby what he himself intends to do (invade a country) is mapped against a target enemy so that the Russian people will grasp concretely the necessity of the invasion, which he called a "special operation" designed to "protect the people" in the predominantly Russian-speaking region of Donbas who, according to Putin, "have been facing humiliation and genocide perpetrated by the Kyiv regime." He then called the operational objective a "denazification" of Ukraine. Intertextually, this is a coded term, intended to evoke the memory of the Soviet Union's defense against Nazi Germany during World War II. It is, clearly, a case of doublespeak, linking Nazism with antisemitism so as to produce a dissonant image in the mind, given Ukraine was led by a Jewish president.

As mentioned, the expression "big lie" was coined by Adolf Hitler in *Mein Kampf* (Chapter 1), to describe the emotional power of fabricating a lie so "colossal" that no one would believe that its perpetrator "could have the impudence to distort the truth so infamously." Hitler's own big lie of an Aryan race that was superior to all other races showed how mind-altering such lying can be, since he used it constantly in his speeches and official pronouncements, destroying social harmony under the false guise of restoring it. To back up his big lie, he used techniques that have now become almost routine on social media—conspiracy theories (against the Jews), fake news (to keep his audiences misinformed, claiming that Germany was not defeated in 1918, but betrayed internally), and false myths (such as the one of a mythic superior race destined by history to rule the world)—which accumulated in people's minds so as to alter official accounts of Germany's history, no doubt providing a justification to the overthrow of Germany's political system at the time. In recent times, the same term has been applied to Donald Trump's attempts to overturn his election loss in the United States. Trump's big lie refers to the false claim that the election was "rigged" and "stolen" from him through massive electoral fraud. Significantly, he also supported his big lie with the same pattern of conspiracy theories and fake news reported on far-right social media platforms, such as QAnon, that instructed Trump supporters to attack the US Capitol on January 6, 2021.

The central aim of all big lies is deception or deceit, as Hobbes and Nietzsche warned in their attack on the political use of metaphor (Chapter 1). Hobbes saw this as the essential quality of metaphor, even claiming that one cannot escape its use when discussing most things including metaphor itself. It is the very nature of metaphor, Hobbes (1656) argued, that implies inherent deceit since it involves "speaking of one thing instead of another." Deception can also involve non-verbal metaphors and symbols, used to reinforce the big lie, such as the Nazi swastika, Trump flags and hats, etc. Without these, lies would not spread as broadly and become embedded into the minds of believers as being true. Disinformation is part of the "big lie game," spread today mainly through the internet and especially social media networks—it can be so realistic and persuasive that it might attract large groups of people to follow the disinformer. In effect, the ultimate goal of political mendacity is the manipulation of minds, through mappings of powerful source domains onto discourse frames and symbolism, which create alternate realities that people may not recognize as false. As Walter Lippmann (1913: 516) put it: "Ours is a problem in which deception has become organized and strong; where truth is poisoned at its source; one in which the skill of the shrewdest brains is devoted to misleading a bewildered people." Already in the 1920s—the post-World War I era—Lippmann was worried about the flood of disinformation and lies that dominated the new mediated environment of newspapers and the radio, because he saw it as allowing political lies to flourish. These, he suggested, gained their emotional power because they disconnected language from reality, turning it on itself into deceptive constructions: "If the connection between reality and human response were direct and immediate, rather than indirect and inferred, indecision and failure would be unknown" (Lippmann 1922: 24). Lippmann illustrates his assertion with the sixth-century case of the Alexandrian monk Cosmas, who aimed to disprove the fact that the planet was spherical. He did this by constructing his own map, not based on relevant geophysical facts but on the basis of his beliefs and feelings. As Lippmann (1920: 55) concluded: "The only feeling that anyone can have about an event he does not experience is the feeling aroused by his mental image of that event. That is why until we know what others think they know, we cannot truly understand their acts."

Political liars play on the same evocation and manipulation of image schemas that produce lasting "pictures in the head," as Lippmann (1922: 34) described them (Chapter 1):

> Those features of the world outside which have to do with the behavior of other human beings, in so far as that behavior crosses ours, is dependent upon us, or is interesting to us, we call roughly public affairs. The pictures inside the heads of these human beings, the pictures of themselves, of others, of their needs, purposes, and relationship, are their public opinions. Those pictures which are acted upon by groups of people, or by individuals acting in the name of groups, are Public Opinion with capital letters.

In other words, people tend to instinctively partake in willful blindness, attending only to those facts which corroborate their existing models of reality. The political liar is thus a master psychologist, who understands the proclivities of the human mind and how to take advantage of them. Propaganda, Lippmann goes on to remark, creates realities that people are not able to recognize as false or as self-serving projections—as we saw with Mussolini, Lenin, and Putin (among many others). For Lippmann, propaganda and stereotypes—a term that he himself coined—have the same cognitive origin: first, people look at an event or person in the world; second, they create a mental picture of that event or person; and third, they respond to the picture, and not to the actual person or event. Political liars know intuitively how to affect the second step, influencing the picture and thus also the answer. They do so, as argued here, by framing the event via metaphorical mapping processes that are projected back and forth to create alternate realities. The ultimate effect of such mind illusions, as Jacques Ellul (1965) called them, is the control of belief.

Lippmann went on to call the manufactured image schemas as "fictions," which are subtle deformations of reality (Lippmann 1922: 57):

> By fictions I do not mean lies ... A work of fiction may have almost any degree of fidelity, and so long as the degree of fidelity can be taken into account, fiction is not misleading ... For the real environment is altogether too big, too complex, and too fleeting for direct acquaintance. We are not equipped to deal with so much subtlety, so much variety, so many permutations and combinations. And although we have to act in that environment, we have to reconstruct it on a simpler model before we can manage with it. To traverse the world men must have maps of the world. Their persistent difficulty is to secure maps on which their own need, or someone else's need, has not sketched in the coast of Bohemia.

The Korzybski Effect

The last comment by Lippmann leads us back to the theoretical doorstep of Alfred Korzybski (1933: 58) who coined the phrase "the map is not the territory it represents," by which he meant overall that thought is impossible to examine independently of language. Language provides maps of reality (the territory), which implies that we interpret the latter in terms of the former. In a way, big lies can be seen as the strategy of using devious metaphorical maps to redesign the normal territories they represent in honest, ethical language, thus distorting the relation between map (words) and territory (conventional meaning) that honest language aims to provide. As Korzybski asserted, this is a result of the tendency of people to confuse maps with territories, that is, representations of reality with reality itself. Language is also how we map internal (beliefs and feelings) modes of understanding to reality, giving them specific structural (linguistic) forms (Korzybski (1933: 20):

> The only link between the verbal and objective world is exclusively structural, necessitating the conclusion that the only content of all "knowledge" is structural. Now structure can be considered as a complex of relations, and ultimately as multi-dimensional order. From this point of view, all language can be considered as names for unspeakable entities on the objective level, be it things or feelings, or as names of relations.

As Hobbes realized, discussing metaphor invariably requires metaphor. To say that the specific well-chosen word "switches the mind on," as suggested here, is clearly a metaphor utilizing the source domain of electric circuitry mapped onto the target domain of mentality. But, as Hobbes, Nietzsche, Korzybski, Lakoff, and many others have cogently argued, this is how we make invisible worlds (abstractions, ideas, etc.) visible in the mind. It is in this metaphorical frame that phrases such as the "Korzybski effect" are located.

Korzybski was clearly aware that the fit between language and reality is bidirectional—that is, it can be used to reflect reality directly (as in literal language), or it can change reality. It is the latter mode of linguistic mapping that produces a Korzybski effect, which can then turn on "mental switches," from disgust (as we saw with the dog biscuits anecdote) to hate, achieved by metaphorical framings that are based on manipulation of meaning, distorting the map-territory relation deviously. As Lakoff (2017) has aptly commented on this type of language:

> All thought is carried out by neural circuitry—it does not float in air. Language neurally activates thought. Language can thus change brains, both for the better and the worse. Hate speech changes the brains of those hated for the worse, creating toxic stress, fear and distrust—all physical, all in one's neural circuitry active every day. This internal harm can be even more severe than an attack with

a fist. It imposes on the freedom to think and therefore act free of fear, threats, and distrust. It imposes on one's ability to think and act like a fully free citizen for a long time.

Metaphors of hate, including those framed by big lies, thus activate "neural circuitry" which can become "hard wired" and thus lead to the acceptance of falsehoods as truths. Lakoff also saw how metaphor can be used (deceptively) to fill in gaps of thought, that may come up when someone does not know *le mot juste* (the appropriate word). The big liar fills the gaps via deceit. The term hypocognition, coined by Robert Levy (1975), refers to the inability to communicate certain ideas because there are no words for them or because someone cannot find the words. Lakoff (2004: 54) used this notion to describe political progressives in the United States, saying that, in comparison to conservatives, they suffer from "massive hypocognition." When someone is hypocognitive, it is easy for the master liar to intervene and fill-in the gap. As Wu and Dunning (2018) have argued, it is hard to recognize what is going on because it is invisible. Long before cognitive linguistics, a creative narrative experiment in hypocognition can be found in Lewis Carroll's poem, titled the *Jabberwock*, which he included in *Through the Looking-Glass, and What Alice Found There* (Carroll 1871). In it, many of the words are nonsensical, even though they possess English word structure; however, Lewis claimed, these are necessary to fill existing gaps in English vocabulary: for example, *brillig* means (according to Humpty Dumpty in the novel) "four o'clock in the afternoon, which is the time when broiling things for dinner takes place;" *wabe* is defined by Alice as "the grass-plot around a sundial," to which Humpty Dumpty retorts, "Of course, it is," because it "goes a long way before it, and a long way behind it."

Regardless of empirical evidence that big lies are just that—lies—they are difficult to eradicate from people's minds, because they produce the Korzybski effect, turning on belief switches, which are virtually impossible to turn off, as psychologist Frederik Lund (1925: 163) has remarked:

> Belief has a large emotional content … there is a marked tendency to idealize the rational principle and to conceive of it as the most valid and important of belief determinants, notwithstanding the fact that non-rational factors appear to outweigh it so largely in conditioning our belief-attitudes. The fact that beliefs once formed are not willingly relinquished is definitely related to, if not responsible for the fact, that the side of the question first presented to us, and the first influences brought to bear upon us, are most effective in determining our beliefs, so much so as to suggest the presence of a law of primacy in persuasion. Belief, as a certain mental content, is present throughout the scale of knowledge and opinion, just as is temperature on a scale the extremes of which are hot and cold; it is not present with the same strength, however, but with varying admixtures of doubt.

The ancient Greek philosophers divided belief into *pistis* and *doxa*. The former implies a sense of trust in something, and the latter a system of opinions that guide actions and behaviors no matter what the truth of the matter. In belief, there are only binary choices—something is either true or false, right or wrong, moral or immoral. In a series of essays titled *Illustrations of the Logic of Science*, the American pragmatist philosopher, Charles S. Peirce (2014), described belief as something that impels us to act, not just a state of mind. He defined it as something that we easily adopt to counteract doubt (the opposite of belief), from which we struggle to free ourselves. In other words, belief is the emotional strategy we use to eliminate the burden of doubt, and mendacious language is the vehicle used by master liars to aid us cunningly in the elimination process.

Epilogue

Deconstructing politically motivated lies using conceptual metaphor theory is a straightforward mode of analysis, as I have attempted to show in this chapter. The reason why this is so is that thought itself may be the result of mappings of various kinds and at different levels of complexity (as will be discussed subsequently). So the deconstruction mirrors in reverse how the object of study (the conceptual metaphorical process) is constructed.

Returning to Dr. King's speech one last time, it is relevant to note that his final set of metaphors, those based on music and sounds, can be seen to constitute a synesthetic balance to his other visual metaphors, thus combining audition with visuality to produce an "aesthetics of thought" that is, arguably, the unconscious source of the emotional power of his speech, which he ended with the metaphor of a ringing bell, using the expression, "let freedom ring," derived from the national song, "My Country 'Tis of Thee," which served as the *de facto* national anthem of the United States before the adoption of "The Star-Spangled Banner" in 1931. In the song, bells echo across the country, both as spiritual sounds and a signals of urgency: "And when this happens, when we allow freedom to ring, when we let it ring from every village and every hamlet, from every state and every city, we will be able to speed up that day when all of God's children, black men and white men, Jews and Gentiles, Protestants and Catholics, will be able to join hands and sing in the words of the old Negro spiritual, 'Free at last! Free at last! Thank God Almighty, we are free at last!'" The auditory image schema is clearly a powerful synesthetic one because the ringing of bells spurs on people to act, joining hands on the journey to social justice and freedom.

It is fitting to conclude this chapter with another statement made by King in another context. When asked why he put up with the lies that were being hurled at him, he responded "No lie can live forever (cited in King 1965)." Dictatorships come and go, confirming the veracity of Luther King's aphorism. The falsehoods on which Soviet Communism, Fascism, and Nazism were based were eventually exposed by the force of truth and objective facts. The false "pictures in the mind" that liars imprint in many people for opportunistic reasons (to use Lippmann's phrase again) will eventually dissipate by themselves. While this may seem to be an idealistic view, history teaches us that King is right—honest political discourse eventually supersedes the falsity of manipulative discourse, which is eventually unmasked as the machinations of the master liar. To cite Senator Patrick Moynihan's admonition: "Everyone is entitled to his own opinion, but not to his own facts" (cited in Moynihan 2010).

3

DA VINCI CODE EFFECTS

Prologue

In 2003, the novel, *The Da Vinci Code*, by American author Dan Brown became an international bestseller and popular culture phenomenon. The hero, a Harvard scholar named Robert Langdon, solves an intriguing historical mystery connecting Jesus and Mary Magdalene in ways that went against the official story of their relationship by the Church—namely that Jesus and Mary had married and went on to have children. Given that it was translated into many languages, and turned into a movie in 2006, it unwittingly instilled into people across the world the belief that conspiracies are real, and that truth is hidden from view by powerful institutions and nefarious political actors. While conspiracism existed before the novel, it is hardly coincidental that it started to spread broadly as a perceived mode of "uncovering the truth" after the novel and movie became a worldwide sensation, moving to the universe of social media, where it has congealed as a powerful genre of virtual discourse, and where conspiracy theory groups, such as QAnon, are born for no other reason than to spread falsehoods, promoting alternative views of history and reality—a mindset that can be called the "Da Vinci Code effect." This can be defined as the view which emerges from belief in conspiracy theories that the truth and real history are hidden from everyone by cabals and secret societies operating behind the social scenes.

In the novel, Langdon attempts to set the historical record right by claiming that Jesus and Mary Magdalene were involved romantically and raised a family, doing so by using his knowledge of "symbology," which the novel defines as the study of signs and symbols. A large part of the allure of that novel comes, arguably, from Langdon's ability to interpret the signs of the purported mystery in the same tradition of great fictional detectives. The truth, Langdon discovers, is concealed in an

DOI: 10.4324/9781003349143-3

enigmatic code, called the "Da Vinci Code," which Langdon ultimately decodes by interpreting the individual clues pertaining to its meaning scattered throughout the plot. To make his story as verisimilar as possible, Brown introduced a neologism, the cryptex, to denote a portable cylinder where secret messages are hidden. He described it as "five doughnut-sized disks of marble that had been stacked and affixed to one another within a delicate brass framework" (Brown 2003: 47). The cylinder works like a combination lock, recalling the ancient scytales of Greek secret writing, thus reinforcing the novel's overall cryptographic, conspiracy theory style and making the "discovery" more believable, since "science" is purportedly used to expose the truth.

This chapter will look at the nature of conspiracy theories and how they are used to produce the Da Vinci Code effect by political liars, an effect that complements the Korzybski effect. The latter refers to the power of metaphors to switch beliefs on, the former to the power of narratives to do the same. Cognitive linguistic analysis in this case involves deconstructing narratives as based on the same pattern of mapping image schemas and source domains—journeys, paths, etc.—onto the conspiratorial texts making them appear coherent and logical.

Conspiracy Thinking

The *Da Vinci Code* exemplifies what a conspiracy theory is essentially about—a well-constructed falsehood that holds together thematically, designed to produce a strong belief in its premises, thus blocking any logical counterargument, no matter what the facts may be. Belief is reinforced and embedded into cognition by apophenia—a term coined by psychiatrist Klaus Conrad in 1958, which he defined as the ingrained tendency to perceive meaningful connections between unrelated things—characterized as "connecting the dots" in Chapter 1, itself a metaphor denoting the compulsion to associate ideas or clues with each other, in order to uncover the "big picture," even when there is no such picture other than in the imagination. Conrad saw apophenia, in fact, as the "unmotivated seeing of connections accompanied by a specific feeling of abnormal meaningfulness." The underlying overall conceptual construct in apophenic dot-connection is the source domain that can be formulated as *"true history is hidden"*, which is mapped against virtually all politically motivated conspiracy theories, such as the "denazification" one used by Putin to justify his invasion of Ukraine (Chapter 2). Conrad uses the term *apophany* to characterize the "aha" moment when a conspiratorial narrative appears to unveil a truth, as in Brown's novel. Unlike an *epiphany*, the experience of a sudden and striking real insight, an apophany is a false insight, produced by the Da Vinci Code effect. As psychologist Peter Brugger (2001) characterized it, apophenia is the "pervasive tendency to see order in random configurations," which congeals into a false or illusory "revelation."

Dan Brown's novel was designed to engender an apophany at the end, after Langdon connected the clues that led to a secret code, which he cleverly associated with the victimization endured by women in the past. As mentioned, the code, after being cracked, revealed that Mary Magdalene was the wife of Jesus who carried his baby (the Holy Grail), surviving evil forces within the Church that have attempted throughout the ages to suppress this fact. All throughout the novel Brown makes reference to "scholarly research" suggesting that Mary and Jesus were romantic partners. But there is no such research, just baseless and spurious conjectures by conspiracy theorists. Guided by the *true history is hidden* metaphorical frame, apophenia is put in motion by clues in the novel.

The code that Langdon decrypts becomes the source of a related conspiracy theory, namely that *cabals run the world*. This can be called a "central governing metaphor" (discussed further subsequently), defined as a "meta-metaphor" from which others are derived. This metaphor is found throughout the social media universe today, where even a scientific occurrence, such as a pandemic, is attributed to the machinations of sinister and powerful groups working behind the scenes, often political in motivation, to control people according to their whims. Trump's deep state metaphor is another derivative from the central metaphor, which, in the case of the coronavirus pandemic is used to explain how political entities behind the scene may have generated it in order to produce negative views of Trump so as to ultimately defeat him at the polls. Central metaphors are so deeply embedded that they allow for derivatives to resist opposition and counterarguments. As the Dan Brown novel showed, once we are drawn into the apophenic system, we start to see the conspiracies as real. During the coronavirus pandemic, politics became a major target of the conspiracists, guided by the central metaphor. This produced a Da Vinci Code effect, which like the Korzybski effect, affects neural circuitry, which, in turn, becomes an impulse to action, such as antivaccine protests and refusal to wear protective masks. The neuroscientific evidence to support this explanation is now abundant. An example is the study on the effects of lying to the brain by Yin and Weber (2019), who investigated the neural mechanisms involved in lying and conspiracism, coming to the conclusion that they might vary subjectively, but are still controlled by specific neural regions (Yin and Weber 2019: 1101):

> To advance our understanding of the underlying neural mechanisms of this heterogeneity, we investigated individual differences in self-serving lying. We performed a functional magnetic resonance imaging study in 37 participants and introduced a color-reporting game where lying about the color would in general lead to higher monetary payoffs but would also be punished if get caught. At the behavioral level, individuals lied to different extents. Besides, individuals who are more dishonest showed shorter lying response time, whereas no significant correlation was found between truth-telling response time and the degree of dishonesty. At the neural level, the left caudate, ventromedial prefrontal cortex (vmPFC), right inferior frontal gyrus (IFG), and left dorsolateral prefrontal cortex (dlPFC) were key regions reflecting individual differences in making dishonest decisions. The dishonesty associated activity in these regions decreased

with increased dishonesty. Subsequent generalized psychophysiological interaction analyses showed that individual differences in self-serving lying were associated with the functional connectivity among the caudate, vmPFC, IFG, and dlPFC. More importantly, regardless of the decision types, the neural patterns of the left caudate and vmPFC during the decision-making phase could be used to predict individual degrees of dishonesty. The present study demonstrated that lying decisions differ substantially from person to person in the functional connectivity and neural activation patterns which can be used to predict individual degrees of dishonesty.

Because conspiracy theories resist falsification, reinforced by factors such as confirmation bias, one of the negative legacies of the covid-19 pandemic has been to spread the Da Vinci Code effect to many other areas of politics, engendering a widespread distrust of authority and the spread of political cynicism. Once limited to fringe groups or individuals, this type of discourse has become commonplace in social media, showing the power of central metaphors to produce apophenic thinking. As Sauter (2017) has remarked, social media and the internet are an "apophenic machine," whereby "one thing leads to another, always another link leading you deeper into nothing and no place, floating through self-dividing and transmogrifying sites until you are awash in the sheer evidence that the internet exists." The following statement by Sauter is, in effect, a supporting acknowledgment that the central metaphor of cabals operating behind the scenes is the overarching mental map behind most political conspiracy theories online:

> Because the conspiratorial mode in part aims to re-center *people* as the evil geniuses of global systems—and as potential heroic saviors—powerful people never do anything that's strictly personal. Because they are meant to serve as avatars of agency, everything they do must have broader relevance, and is available ultimately to be mixed and matched in our filter-bubble realities. Everything they do must refer back to their conspiratorial roles, so their lives are understood as Machiavellian at all levels, always concerned with concealment and secret keeping. In denying these perceived power players their private lives, the conspiratorial mode also denies them human, emotional responses to the events around them.

Every society tells of its historical origins through stories that allow the members of a collectivity to understand the *raison d'être* of their institutions, beliefs, laws, languages and cultural systems. Story-tellers are thus powerful "meaning-makers," because they are the ones who take the "facts" of history and assemble them into a narrative that provides a sense of meaningful connectivity to a society's antecedent events. So, the way a historical narrative is written or told shapes the way people envision history itself. It is little wonder therefore that, in Orwell's novel, historical narration is controlled by the Ministry of Truth, which shapes the facts to fit the Party's worldview. The historical records are thus written in doublespeak to produce an "alternative history" guided by a central metaphor created by the Ministry of Truth—*deniers of the alternative history are "unpersons."* The protagonist of the novel, Winston Smith, works in the Records Department of the Ministry of Truth. His job is to revise historical records in order to ensure that any account of the past conforms to the party line, deleting any inconvenient facts perpetrated by "unpersons," that is, by those who oppose the state and whose memory of the facts must be denied or eliminated by "vaporization." The idea is to obfuscate real events, including those that are linked to personal histories. The description of Smith's birthday is a case-in-point: "It was a bright cold day in April, and the clocks were striking thirteen" (Orwell 1959: 3). This implies that the factual date of his birth remains uncertain, leaving him in a mind fog. The same type of uncertainty characterizes the spinning of conspiracy theories, which are deliberately vague and allusive, allowing any self-styled political Ministry of Truth to control people's understanding of past events. As Orwell understood, such political institutions allow totalitarian regimes to spin their own historical "truths" that shield them from the opposition. This very strategy was used by Stalin to silence the opposition against him, keeping people in a state of fear and uncertainty; Vladimir Putin has used the same tactic in order to maintain power, claiming that there is an international conspiracy against Russia by those who oppose its mission and goals.

Creating alternative narratives was a key strategy used by Trump throughout his presidency. He deployed the "deep state" metaphor to spin his false conspiratorial theories—a metaphor based on the central metaphor of a cabal (above). The deep state is, in fact, portrayed as a clique of liberal politicians and intellectuals who had the reins of power before Trump came to power and who, behind the scenes, continue to plot against him because they fear that he will expose them. This conspiracy works for many people because it claims to tell the "real story" of the overtaking of America by "un-American" liberals—a version of Orwell's "unpersons." Like the "truth" hidden in the Da Vinci Code, the deep state metaphor works on the mind below the threshold of detection—hence the use of "deep" to frame the conspiracy. Its believability is strengthened by what Korzybski (1921) called time-binding, in reference to how our sense of history is reflected constantly in the structure of our languages and our narratives.

The deep state metaphor actually crystallized in America before Trump—who simply co-opted it for his own objectives. In 1993, Peter Dale Scott published *Deep Politics and the Death of JFK*, in which he claimed that the JFK assassination unlocked a Pandora's box of issues kept hidden from the public's view, highlighting the purported role of nefarious clandestine political actors who benefited from the assassination. In other words, it was a deep state that was behind the JFK assassination, and it is to the same cabal that Trump and others have attributed many subsequent events, including the supposed staging of 9/11 and the creation of a virus to spread a pandemic that subserved the cabal's aim to bring Trump down. Used constantly by QAnon and other conspiracists, the deep state metaphor alludes to corruption in government that can only be combatted by Trump. As such, the metaphor does several things at once—it taps into a spreading belief among many that liberalism and its elitist discourse has ensconced itself "deeply" into American politics and society at large and thus needs to be eradicated, at the same time that it fits in with the conspiratorial narrative of persecution that Trump is always spreading to protect himself from political opposition and even legal actions—persecution from the political left. Trump has repeated this metaphor so many times, in public and in tweets, that it has become a Korzybskian linguistically-altered map.

When someone pieces together random news clippings and decides, for instance, that the 9/11 terrorist attacks were an inside job, that person is engaging in apo-phenic thinking, connecting the news clips as clues and then mapping them against the target domain of a conspiracy behind the scenes. Conspiracy theories used by political opportunists do the dot-connecting for followers, so that they can control the apophenic process. Trump's ability to concoct and spread conspiracy theories like the deep state one has been a source of apophenia throughout the US and likely the world, allowing conspiratorial thinking to gain traction, shaping everyday stream of consciousness—a term introduced by William James (1890) to explain how thought flows and how language and narratives provide a channel for the stream to flow towards meaning-making. History is a narrative channel for directing the flow in a certain way. The same kind of channeling is employed by conspiracy narratives based on big lies. Hitler spinned his Aryan race narrative to channel people's beliefs towards an antisemitic direction; Trump used deep state conspira-cies in a similar way to deflect attention away from himself and towards the cabal operating behind the scenes. In effect, Hitler, Trump, and other big liars rewrite history according to their own Orwellian-type account. After Obama came to power, Trump perpetrated and perpetuated his false "birther" conspiracy theory that Obama was not born in the US, thus intimating by suggestion that Obama was a part of an international deep state cabal. During his presidency he perpetrated all kinds of conspiracy theories, knowing full well that these would channel some people's consciousness in a self-serving direction, culminating in his big lie that the 2020 election was stolen from him by elements in the deep state—a lie that galvanized his voter base. Such conspiracies have allowed Trump to instill apophenia broadly, as evidenced by the spread of multiple conspiracy theories based on this central meta-phor, namely that the world is run by one vast cabal operating in secrecy.

Often it is the Jewish people who are identified as the leaders of the cabal—hence the plethora of antisemitic conspiracies that have resisted dismantling. Since at least the Middle Ages, Jews have been accused of everything from poisoning wells and causing the death of Jesus to starting the bubonic plague. Perhaps the most per-nicious of these is the falsehood that they are behind a plot to control the world. As mentioned in Chapter 1, evidence for this plot is found apophenically everywhere, showing how the Da Vinci Code effect works, guiding the concoction of false narratives such as the belief that the Jews are behind international banking schemes, Hollywood, the news media, etc. Perhaps the most ludicrous of all conspiracy theories is the one perpetrated by English media personality David Icke (2007) who claims that an inter-dimensional race of reptilian beings has hijacked the Earth, creating a genetically modified hybrid race of reptilian "shape shifter" cabals, which include the Babylonian Brotherhood, the Illuminati, and other elite cabals who fabricate events to keep humans in fear. The absurdity of this theory has not stopped countless people from accepting it as true, especially since Icke uses it to stoke antisemitic beliefs, identifying numerous Jewish political figures as reptilian shape shifters. His absurd, laughable theory is made believable to some because it resonates with apocalyptic overtones and allusions.

The origins of apophenia may be evolutionary according to some psychologists—hence its presence as a cognitive force in everyday life as a mechanism for deducing patterns, even when they may not be real or even realistic. Seeking patterns is at the core of mathematics and science, and other knowledge-making activities. This comes from the evolutionary fact that we are programmed to find links and attach meaning to observable events and processes. However, the same mechanism is apparently behind the tendency to connect random or disparate events as meaningful, even when they are not.

Conspiracy Theories

A study by Tangherini et al. (2020) looked at how conspiracy theories emerge and spread online, providing relevant insights into how they meld random facts and misinformation cohesively into a narrative framework that coheres into a type of Da Vinci Code logic. The researchers examined the spread of conspiracy theories such as "Pizzagate," about a Washington, D. C. pizza eatery—the Comet Ping Pong Pizzeria—that was claimed to be the hub of a child sex-trafficking ring involving prominent Democratic Party officials, including Hillary Clinton. The researchers found that the narrative form itself emerged from the connections that were united like threads holding a fabric together. The researchers found that the Pizzagate narrative arose from an apopheniac interpretation of hacked emails released in 2016 by Wikileaks, and other bits of information scattered throughout social media, including those connected to the central metaphor of the cabal. Analyzing nearly 18,000 posts from April 2016 through February 2018 on social media sites, the researchers were able to unravel layers of false threads that would come untangled if just one, such as the Wikileaks thread, was removed from the narrative. It is no coincidence that this conspiracy led to the rise of QAnon, which became its main perpetrator.

As mentioned (Chapter 1), QAnon is a conspiracy theory machine that emerged online, whose followers search for clues of conspiracies everywhere dropped by a mysterious individual identified as Q. The group is sustained by the central metaphor of a cabal of satanic, cannibalistic abusers of children conspiring against Donald Trump—the purported savior of the world. From this, QAnon derives pseudo-religious metaphors and symbols, such as the "calm before the storm," which alludes to divine punishment of the cabal and a purification of the world. Aware of the influence of QAnon on his followers, on October 5, 2017 Trump stood beside a group of military leaders at the White House. At one point he uttered to the reporters present, "You guys know what this represents?", tracing an incomplete circle in the air with his right index finger. When asked what it meant, Trump responded, "Maybe it's the calm before the storm," echoing the QAnon metaphor.

Arguably because of the Da Vinci Code effect and its apparent validity from supporting neuroscientific research (above), conspiracy theories can and do provoke some people to act out in accordance with the false allegations. A citizen actually went to the Washington pizzeria identified by QAnon as the location where child sex trafficking was taking place, with a revolver and a rifle looking for supposed enclaves hiding victims. In courtroom testimony, the gunman claimed that he had read about the story online, watching videos about it, which spurred him to go and investigate the matter himself, with the intent of rescuing the children from harm. This was not the only abnormal response that the Pizzagate conspiracy theory incentivized. In January of 2017, a man from Shreveport, Louisiana, pleaded guilty to making a threatening phone call to Besta Pizza, another pizzeria on the same block as Comet Ping Pong, three days after the previous attack. He had threatened to "save the kids" and "finish what the other guy didn't." In January of 2019, Comet Ping Pong suffered an arson attack that was described on social media as "finishing the job."

What this reveals is that the brain can be manipulated apophenically via the mapping of conspiratorial source domains onto targets of self-serving interest, allowing the conspiracists to provide illusory evidence that they see as corroborative of the central conspiracy. Political manipulators know how to take advantage of this ingrained tendency, both spinning and appropriating conspiracy theories advantageously. An example of appropriation emerged during the covid-19 pandemic, when conspiracy groups such as QAnon spun a false narrative about political entities working behind the scenes, producing the virus so that Trump's voter favorability would fall. As a result, those who subscribed to the conspiracy theory reacted by seeing protective masks and vaccines as political symbols, rather than prophylactic devices against the spread and persistence of the virus. It is no coincidence that Trump himself refused to wear a mask, in support of the conspiracy theory, even though he eventually caught the virus and was hospitalized. Politics outdoes common sense when it is guided by unconscious metaphorical structures.

Such conspiratorial reactions are not however unique in history, as already discussed in reference to the Dreyfus affair. In his 1742 novel, *Journal of the Plague Year,* Daniel Defoe described the mass panic that common people experienced as they tried to come to grips with the bubonic plague, doing so by spinning false stories about its origins. The novel recounts how news of a frightening disease took grip of people in Holland in 1664, reputedly brought to its shores by a Turkish fleet. The illness soon spread to London by unknown means, spawning gossip and speculation about the origins of the disease, including the theory that it was brought to England's shores from ships originating in the French port of Marseilles. His *Journal* is one of the first texts to point the finger at misinformation as the source for the panic and for the unsuccessful outcomes of public health measures to stem the spread of the disease. The fake cures and quack practitioners Defoe describes are also among the first examples of how misinformation and self-interest can hamper and even thwart practical medical intervention, eerily forecasting the false cures bandied about during covid-19. As Umberto Eco (2010: 58) has written, as far back as ancient Greece how people talked about diseases and devised stories about them impelled people to "believe or act in a certain way." Conspiracy theories are clearly not unique to the present era; they surface in times of crisis, no matter what form they take. However, never before in human history have they become so widespread and politically motivated as during modernity, when Machiavellian political actors, from Stalin and Hitler to Trump and Putin have had at their disposal the channels of mass communications to spread them to their advantage. It is the massiveness of diffusion that such channels permit that has added to the perceived plausibility of the misinformation, given that, as any widely accepted belief, it is difficult emotionally to go against the grain. Moreover, the feeling of participation whereby people on social media not only accept the meaning of a conspiracy theory at face value, but add to it subjectively by commenting on it through personal posts, strengthens the believability factor—that is, the conspiratorial system (one textual version based on another and on another and so on) makes the false ideas even more believable in themselves. It is at such points of diffusion that a conspiracy theory becomes impervious to falsification to believers, and any contrary evidence is seen as evidence of the conspiracy itself.

Significantly, the term *conspiracy theory* was coined by the Central Intelligence Agency in 1967 in reference to the many unfounded theories about the JFK assassination that were spreading throughout America after his death. As Anna Merlan (2019) has insightfully remarked:

> The reality is that the US has been a nation gripped by conspiracy for a long time. The Kennedy assassination has been hotly debated for years. The feminist and antiwar movements of the 1960s were, for a time, believed by a not-inconsiderable number of Americans to be part of a communist plot to weaken the country. A majority have believed for decades that the government is hiding what it knows about extraterrestrials. There is a perpetual tug between conspiracy theorists and actual conspiracies, between things that are genuinely not believable and truths that are so outlandish they can be hard, at first, to believe. But while conspiracy theories are as old as the US itself, there is something new at work; historically, times of tumult and social upheaval tend to lead to a parallel surge in conspiracy thinking; our increasingly rigid class structure, one that leaves many people feeling locked into their circumstances. Together, these elements helped create a society in which many Americans see millions of snares, laid by a menacing group of enemies, all the more alarming for how difficult they are to identify and pin down.

Pinning down the source of a conspiracy narrative is becoming truly impossible, given that it can become part of a digital discourse system, characterized by hashtags, chat groups, and Google searches. In this virtual environment, believers develop their own language, called a "plandemic," which imparts a sense of truth to the cabal metaphor. The term "plandemic" is traced to a 2020 conspiracy theory video, *Plandemic: The Hidden Agenda Behind Covid-19* and the related film, *Plandemic: Indoctrination*, which promoted misinformation about the coronavirus pandemic as something "planned" behind the scenes. The video went viral and became embedded in the minds of many as believable. The notion of a secret "plan," as discussed with respect to antisemitic conspiracy theories, has become a widespread one via the internet, spread mainly by influential online conspiracists and conspiratorial groups such as QAnon. The plan can be supposedly uncovered by connecting the clue dots left by Q, much like Langdon did to unravel the Da Vinci Code by connecting clues in the novel. Incidentally, the links between Brown's novel and QAnon should not be ignored, as Adam Lewental (2020) has plausibly reasoned. As he insightfully remarks:

> How can so many disregard the clear and obvious facts printed in mainstream media in order to believe in an improbably vast conspiracy [QAnon]? For the same reasons that they fell in love with "The Da Vinci Code" 17 years ago. A palace intrigue of epic proportions. Codes and puzzles hidden in plain sight, with a mysterious man acting as the augur. A shadowy organization involved in dark rituals with global stakes. And you, reader, are breathlessly tasked with solving the riddle in real time, using the clues, your natural intuition, and perhaps your internet search engine of choice.

As he goes on to emphasize, the QAnon phenomenon "is exactly a Dan Brown plot, where dumb and obvious codes are meant to mimic intellectualism." Conspiracists do not want to be told what to believe; rather they use the "critical thinking" exemplified by Robert Langdon, which is hardly that, but rather, the result of an apophenic effect generated by a "dopamine rush of being in the know, of solving the challenging, obscure puzzle."

In this area, the ideas of political scientist Michael Barkun (2003) seem relevant. Barkun sees conspiracism as motivated by three main reasons: first, conspiracy theories emerge to explain what institutional-scientific analysis cannot, thus, they come forward to allow people to make sense out of something that is otherwise confusing, which is, paradoxically, a function of ancient mythology (discussed further in Chapter 5); second, they do so in an appealingly simple way, dividing the world between the forces of light and the forces of darkness, which is a central metaphor in cultures across the world; and third, they are often presented as special, secret knowledge unknown or unappreciated by others, a style that clearly imitates the fictional one used by Dan Brown. As Lewental emphasized, the latter reason gives believers a sense of powerful knowledge that allows them to feel that they have uncovered a mystery. As Barkun (2003: 3) puts it: "For conspiracy theorists, the masses are a brainwashed herd, while the conspiracy theorists in the know can congratulate themselves on penetrating the plotters' deceptions."

An example of how a political manipulator can tap into this kind of mass psychology and twist it to his favor is Trump's creation of the MAGA (Make America Great Again) conspiracy narrative. On the surface, it seems simply to evoke an image of an idyllic past, free from the moral relativism of postmodernism that many feel had beset America under previous presidencies, especially the presidency of Barack Obama. But below this surface it is a code, revolving around a phobia of anyone who does not fit in with MAGA. Like Dan Brown, Trump leaves clues everywhere, aided by conspiracists such as QAnon, of the deterioration of the "real America." As a skilled Machiavellian deceiver, Trump realized from the outset of his campaign to become president that he could tap into this conspiracist mindset, starting with his "birther" claim that Obama was in reality a Muslim and was not born in the United States. This had an instant powerful impact on those who were dissatisfied with the style of liberal government that appeared to be imposed on them by Obama and his supporters —which were the "deep state," a metaphor that (as discussed) gained widespread currency after Trump achieved the presidency. The birther falsehood thus stoked an inner sense of resentment, making it virtually immune from counter-argumentation. Attempts to dispel it, in fact, typically go awry, even after Trump begrudgingly admitted that it was not true. He no longer needed this falsehood, since it was easily transferred to the MAGA narrative, which he used consistently at rallies to stir up hatred of the purported liberal members of the deep state. The strategy can be summed up in one of George Orwell's aphorisms: "Let's all get together and have a good hate" (Orwell 2011: 11).

MAGA is coded with many metaphorical meanings. One of these is the war metaphor, constituting a battle cry for change, led by the leader himself, Donald Trump. This strategy recalls Mussolini's cry for a recovery and revival of Italy's great imperial Roman past. Mussolini even used the Roman hand salute at his rallies to evoke the symbolic importance of this past, as well as looking imperiously into the skies by tilting his head sideways and slightly upwards. Trump eerily employs a similar type of gestural symbolism at his rallies, raising his head askew after reciting a falsehood, inciting his followers to perceive him as a warrior chief who has raised the MAGA flag, to symbolize the fight for the "real America." In this frame, Q is seen as an army general working secretly in helping Trump on to victory, encouraging supporters to "Follow the White Rabbit"—an allusion to Lewis Carroll's *Alice in Wonderland* (1865), whereby Alice literally goes down the hole of the White Rabbit, taking her to Wonderland, thus allowing her to enter an alternate universe. This enfolds the journey metaphor into a discovery of truth hidden below the ground, where the "deep state" can be located and can thus be defeated.

Fauconnier and Turner (2002) have argued that when correlations between conceptual constructions, are mapped onto each other, we start to see similarities, such as those that can be established imaginatively between journeys of discovery and journeys leading to victory. Fauconnier and Turner call this a *blending* process involving different mappings that coalesce into one overall meaning—called the stage of *completion*. It can be claimed that this type of multiple mapping processes produce the overall conspiratorial metaphorical code such as the QAnon one of the deep state cabal. As Fauconnier and Turner (2002: 15) put it: "Almost invisibly to consciousness, conceptual blending choreographs vast networks of conceptual meaning, yielding cognitive products that, at the conscious level, appear simple."

Mind Control

Conspiracy theories can become alternate histories revealing the supposedly hidden truth behind events—which is the main narrative technique used by Dan Brown. When taken over by despots, these are catapulted to center stage as the revealed truth, as did Hitler with his Aryan myth, which became, during his tenure as the Führer, the only accepted view of history in Germany. Orwell characterized this false historiographical strategy in terms of his Ministry of Truth, as discussed, a mind-control system based on the use of an alternate history. It is the Ministry, in fact, that produces the historical records, written in doublespeak based on alternative facts derived from a central mythology. Most unfounded conspiracy theories function as alternate histories of some event. As Orwell understood, these allow totalitarian regimes to spin derivative conspiracy theories that shield them from the opposition. As Chaim Sinar (2018) has perceptively observed, this very strategy was used by Stalin to silence the opposition against him (as mentioned briefly), keeping people in a state of fear and uncertainty. Vladimir Putin uses the same type of conspiratorial historiography, whereby there has always been an international attempt to thwart Russia's nationalistic aspirations.

Orwell warned that the rise of totalitarianism was more likely to emerge when language and history are distorted to serve the machinations of the dictator. His description of doublespeak (originally Newspeak) showed how language can be used to suppress free thought by adapting it to the semantic premises in an alternate historiography. Trump achieves a similar kind of "meaning control" by assigning to specific words and phrases a sense and significance that plays constantly on the promotion of the MAGA narrative, allowing him to manipulate meaning in an Orwellian way. His deep state metaphor allows him to characterize those who oppose him as villains—Democrats, liberals, and the media that criticize him, which he describes as "enemies of the people."

The main argument made here is that once Da Vinci Code effects take hold of people the political manipulator can easily put forth his own clues of a cabal against him that are designed to impel followers to find them hidden everywhere. The term "menticide," introduced by Dutch psychiatrist Joost Meerloo (1965), seems to apply to how big liars are able to "kill the mind." Meerloo came up with this notion after experiencing the Nazi occupation of the Netherlands. He defined it as a surrender to conspiracy theories, which alter how ordinary cognition functions.

As Italian philosopher Antonio Gramsci (1947) claimed, human minds are not always swayed by reasoning or by truth, but rather by contradictions and false beliefs. Mind control is thus achieved by the party in power gaining hegemony in all spheres of culture and communication through these contradictions.

As Hitler wrote cynically about big lies in *Mein Kampf*: "The intelligence of the masses is small. Their forgetfulness is great. They must be told the same thing a thousand times." By embedding the same big lie (or the alternative narrative of Aryanism) into doublespeak, Hitler knew that the strategy would lower the critical reasoning levels of his followers, much like a fantasy impels us to suspend disbelief. As media scholar Francesco Mangiapane (2018: 298) has aptly observed, conspiratorial narratives, such as the everyday social posts that communicate them, affect people in this truth-suspending way:

> Almost entirely absent [*from such news sites*] are posts that call for the reader to make an effort to interpret the post or call on their critical abilities. These sites take nothing for granted. Like in *telenovelas* of the past all ambiguity is cancelled out and the tendency is to guide the story through predictable, unproblematic scenarios.

It is relevant to note that the term *propaganda* derives from the Latin name of a group of Roman Catholic cardinals, the *Congregatio de Propaganda Fide* (Congregation for the Propagation of the Faith) established by Pope Gregory XV in 1622 to supervise the missionaries who were tasked to spread Catholicism. Gradually, the word came to mean any effort to spread beliefs of a particular kind. It acquired its political meaning after World War I when journalists exposed the dishonest, but effective, techniques that propagandists had used during the war. In the early 1900s, Lenin argued that propaganda works because it uses half-truths and slogans to arouse the masses, whom he considered incapable of understanding complicated ideas. Stalin, who came to power in the late 1920s, used propaganda to crush the opposition. And in 1933, Adolf Hitler set up his Nazi dictatorship, imposing his own form of propaganda throughout society, stoking racist and xenophobic paranoia among the populace.

Needless to say, democratic governments have also used propaganda; but it would be a false equivalency to compare such usage with that of a Hitler, a Stalin, or a Mussolini. In 1953, the American government established the US Information Agency (USIA) to create support for its foreign policy. The Voice of America, the radio division of the USIA, broadcast entertainment, news, and American-oriented propaganda throughout the world. The government used the Central Intelligence Agency (CIA) to spread sentiments against governments unfriendly to the United States. These included porpagandistic messages against the Soviet Union and the Communist countries of Eastern Europe. The CIA also provided funds to establish radio networks, called Radio Free Europe and Radio Liberty, which broadcast American views and warnings to Communist countries. Without going into the politics of propaganda of this type, suffice it to say here that propaganda on any side of the political spectrum gains believability when ideas are framed in coded metaphorical ways. There is no mind control without semantic control. The problem emerges when propaganda is used benevolently versus propanganda used maliciously, since it is often a matter of differential interpretations. It is the clearly-identifiable malicious type of propaganda, such as the kind used by a Hitler or a Putin, that is of relevance to the present treatment.

Machiavelli saw the concoction of false narratives as a critical tactic in gaining and maintaining political power, writing an entire treatise on them to emphasize their important role in politically-oriented mind control (Machiavelli 1513). The objective is to generate paranoia (as it came to be called after Machiavelli) among as many people as possible, which then spreads to affect virtually everyone, even those who do not believe the conspiracy but may find themselves needing to dispute its veracity, thus adding to the cumulus of paranoia that the conspiracy is designed to evoke. As Machiavelli emphasized, the art of political conspiracy involves, in other words, creating a false narrative in which enemies of the state are portrayed as scheming against it, either from outside or within it, manipulating reality in the process. From this paranoid environment, the Machiavellian leader emerges as a political savior who has come to the rescue.

Geoff Nunberg (2018) has perceptively written that a conspiracy theory, such as the deep state one, is a powerful tool of mind control that is more effective than any other kind of established brainwashing technique because the believer does not feel brainwashed, but as having decoded the truth personally. Psychologist Sander van der Linden (2015) encapsulates this as follows:

Conspiracy theorists rarely simply endorse a single conspiracy theory. Rather, belief in one often serves as evidence for belief in others, and this quickly turns into a worldview, i.e., a lens through which we view the world, with new information about world events processed not according to the weight of the evidence but rather in terms of how consistent it is with one's prior convictions. For example, studies have shown that people who believe in conspiracy theories often espouse mutually contradictory explanations about the same event, and are even eager to endorse entirely made-up conspiracy theories. In sum, it's not really about the actual evidence anymore, but rather about whether a theory is consistent with a larger conspiratorial worldview.

Once drawn in, the victim of a conspiracy theory will tend to interpret and judge events in the world not in an objective way, but in terms of the insinuations of the theory itself. To put it in cognitive linguistic terms when a cluster of mappings are activated to produce a conspiratorial blend, it is virtually impossible to accept that the target of the mappings is false. As George Lakoff has cogently argued, this is so because politically-designed metaphors revolve around a *moral account* image schema that is mapped onto several domains, including the perception of what is moral and what is immoral (for example, Lakoff 2016a). The MAGA theory is embedded in this mapping system, portraying contrasting views of America as immoral, which leads to a belief in an urgent political need for restitution, turning the negative into the positive.

Cognitive Dissonance

The foregoing discussion leads to the notion of cognitive dissonance, a mental syndrome caused by a discord between one's beliefs and contrasting facts. To resolve the dissonance, people will seek out information that confirms their beliefs, avoiding anything that is in conflict with them or else developing strategies that are designed to attenuate the dissonance and even turn the contrasting information on its head, so as to make it fit their beliefs. For this reason, it is unlikely that people with strong convictions will ever change their minds about anything. As Festinger, Riecken, and Schachter (1956: 3) have described it:

> A man with a conviction is a hard man to change. Tell him you disagree and he turns away. Show him the facts or figures and he questions your sources. Appeal to logic and he fails to see your point.

Cognitive dissonance is a mixture of denial and rationalization, a refusal to accept uncomfortable evidence that contradicts embedded beliefs and the deployment of strategies to make contradictory evidence compatible with the beliefs. As Trump supporters came to believe his big lie that the 2020 election was stolen from him, they came to perpetrate it themselves, incapable of accepting the possibility that they could be wrong and thus duped by their leader. This pattern of resistance to the facts that contradict deeply-rooted beliefs has occurred across time—for example, the belief that there was a Jewish conspiracy to control the world, emphasized especially by the Nazis, has resisted time decay and continues to reverberate in neo-Nazi-type groups, where contrary evidence is either dismissed or seen as produced by the Jewish cabal itself.

As is known broadly, cognitive dissonance was first identified when psychologist Leon Festinger (1957) studied a group, called the Seekers, that believed the Earth would be destroyed by a flood on December 21, 1954. The Seekers also believed that they would be rescued by an alien spaceship. On the designated date, the group excitedly waited for the arrival of the craft and their departure. When it did not arrive, they were led to believe that there had been an error in communication, and another date was announced. After subsequent predictions of the flood did not materialize on revised dates, the most committed believers in the group concluded that the Earth was not flooded because of the faithfulness of the group. The less totally committed members adjusted their thinking, concluding that there was a miscommunication or that they did not interpret the prediction correctly. The believers thus either denied or bent reality for the purpose of maintaining their own dignity. They also avoided the possibility that they were bamboozled, which would have been felt as even more destructive personally. These same mental gymnastics are involved with Trump supporters as they confronted a lost election and the rampage of the January 6 insurrection. It allows them to avoid accepting that their belief and involvement in Trump's conspiratorial narrative were based on a falsehood.

People who are duped by con artists, hucksters, or shysters will often remain tacit or incapable of taking action against them, after discovering that they were likely conned. Once a consummate liar is believed, it is almost impossible to see through his lies and accept the truth. The feeling of being duped is so destructive that it is easier to deny the facts or else explain them away in some self-illusory way. In the case of someone who has become invested emotionally in the liar because of deeply held beliefs that he has stoked, then any proof provided against him will actually impel the deceived person to dig in even more, as Festinger, Riecken, and Schachter (1956: 3) found in their studies of cognitive dissonance:

> Suppose an individual believes something with his whole heart; suppose further that he has a commitment to this belief and he has taken irrevocable actions because of it; finally, suppose that he is presented with evidence, unequivocal and undeniable evidence, that his belief is wrong: what will happen? The individual will frequently emerge, not only unshaken, but even more convinced of the truth of his beliefs than ever before. Indeed, he may even show a new fervor for convincing and converting other people to his view.

The social media universe is where cognitive dissonance is resolved on a daily basis—a virtual space where the distinction between truth and mendacity, conspiracy theories and science, facts and alternative facts, no longer holds in any commonly-accepted objective sense. It has produced a state of mind that is constantly involved in resolving cognitive dissonance similar to the strategies used by the Seekers. The world in which cyberspace denizens live is often a cognitively dissonant one. As Neil Postman prefigured in his 1992 book, *Technopoly: The Surrender of Culture to Technology*, when a society becomes reliant on technology, seeking authorization through it and deriving recreation from it, what counts is information in itself, not its real meaning. In this ambiance of mind, cognitive dissonance is constantly at work inducing people to resolve conflicts between fact and fiction, truth and lies, simulation and reality. As internet engineer Jaron Lanier (2010: 12) warned perceptively and ominously:

> We [engineers] make up extensions to your being, like remote eyes and ears (webcams and mobile phones) and expanded memory (the world of details you can search for online). These become the structures by which you connect to the world and other people ... We tinker with your philosophy by direct manipulation of your cognitive experience ... It takes only a tiny group of engineers to create technology that can shape the entire future of human experience with incredible speed.

The internet is where people's minds can be easily "engineered," as Lanier warned. Despite evidence contradicting Trump's big lie, it is perceived as true by followers, who post their conspiracy theories on social media on a constant basis. Like Festinger's Seekers, believers of the big lie had to confront a dissonant situation when Trump lost the election officially, doing so by spreading his lies even more extensively throughout cyberspace. A major difference between the Seekers and Trump supporters is the ability of a falsehood to instantly reach millions of people across the country, making the resolution of dissonance much more facile, since it is believed that so many cannot be wrong—which is how big lies become accepted as true, recalling Hitler's own definition.

Epilogue

Needless to say, not all beliefs are based on conspiracies. Some are real, guiding discovery of facts, and can be either confirmed or rejected objectively. In this sense, beliefs are part of intuition and inference. In Carroll's *Through the Looking-Glass,* the White Queen encapsulates the type of belief system that is susceptible instead to illusions and falsehoods as follows: "Why, sometimes I've believed as many as six impossible things before breakfast." The urgency of unraveling the layers of metaphors that are mapped onto conspiracy theories is of primary relevance today, given the threat that such narratives pose to democracies and other systems based on freedom of thought. Aware of the danger, a podcast called QAnon Anonymous was started in 2018 specifically to debunk conspiracy theories, and especially the QAnon movement, calling it a "big tent conspiracy theory" because of its ability to constantly evolve and add new false claims. One of most bizarre theories under the big tent is that John Kennedy Jr. is the heir to Trump's throne—a conspiracy that in November of 2021 attracted hundreds of QAnon followers to Dealey Plaza in Dallas, the site of JFK's assassination, believing that both Kennedy father and son would show up, proclaiming Trump's reinstatement as president, and that when Trump stepped down Kennedy Jr. would become president. None of this occurred, needless to say. But the believers, like the Seekers, explained it away in various ways, such as the possibility that the time was not right, that the clue left by Q was not deciphered correctly, and so on.

In *The Da Vinci Code*, Langdon receives the assistance of police cryptologist Sophie Neveu, on his quest to find the legendary Holy Grail. A noted British Grail historian in the novel, the fictitious Sir Leigh Teabing, tells them that the location of the Grail is encoded in Leonardo da Vinci's wall painting, *The Last Supper*, which eventually leads the duo to the discovery of the Da Vinci Code. Also searching for the Grail is a secret cabal within the religious community known as Opus Dei, which wants to keep the Grail's location a secret in order to prevent the destruction of Christianity. Prefiguring QAnon, Brown involves the so-called Priory of Sion in the narrative, a fictitiously-created organization founded in France in 1956 by Pierre Plantard so as to create a neo-chivalric order. Plantard claimed that his self-styled order was the latest front for a secret society founded by the crusader Godfrey of Bouillon, on Mount Zion in the Kingdom of Jerusalem in 1099. He further claimed that the Priory was engaged in a centuries-long behind-the-scenes attempt to reveal a secret bloodline of the Merovingian dynasty, which soon became blended with the notion of a Jesus bloodline popularized by the 1982 conspiracy-based book, *The Holy Blood and the Holy Grail* (Baigent, Leigh, and Lincoln 1982). This whole line of conspiracy thinking was incorporated by Dan Brown to make his novel purportedly verifiable historically. Brown's novel promoted the main themes of the Priory theory, but departed from it by portraying the Priory as a mystery cult seeking to restore the feminist theology of early Christianity, which was supposedly suppressed by the Catholic Church. Brown presented this speculation as fact in his preface, as well as in follow-up interviews after the book became a global bestseller.

The Da Vinci Code effect is used here, in sum, to encapsulate how conspiracy theories work and how they twist cognitive and belief mechanisms in the brain. Interestingly and significantly, a research study by Linden (2015) has lent further substance to the validity of this effect. The 316 participants in the study were randomly assigned to one of three groups; (a) those who were shown a brief conspiracy video about global warming, (b) those shown an inspirational pro-climate video, and (c) a control group. The results indicated that those participants who were exposed to the conspiracy video were "significantly less likely to think that there is widespread scientific agreement on human-caused climate change, less likely to sign a petition to help reduce global warming, and less likely to donate or volunteer for a charity in the next six months" (Linden 2015: 171). The overall implication of the study was that "exposure to popular conspiracy theories can have negative and undesirable societal consequences."

4

FAKE NEWS AND PSEUDO-EVENTS

Prologue

In 1833, publisher Benjamin Day founded the *Sun of New York City*, a newspaper that prefigured the so-called penny press trend in American journalism, characterized by sensationalistic reports of crime, celebrities, and unproven feats of pseudo-science. It was the *Sun* that introduced one of the first examples of modern-day journalistic fake news—a series of six articles, starting on August 25, 1835, which purported to report on the discovery of life and civilization on the moon, falsely attributed to British astronomer John Herschel. Subsequently known as the "Great Moon Hoax," the articles were instrumental in making fake news a pattern in journalism and, shortly thereafter, politics. The newspaper's offices were besieged by a horde of people wanting to read more and more about the fake moon story, which according to Edgar Allan Poe was plagiarized from his own tongue-in-cheek story, *The Unparalleled Adventure of One Hans Pfaal* (1835), about a fictitious character named Hans Pfaal who travelled to the moon in a hot air balloon, finding life there and then deciding to live among the moon people.

The *Sun* never retracted the false story, likely because it was profitable, gaining the newspaper a large circulation. An unstated principle for fake news perpetrators, moreover, is that they should never retract anything, denying all evidence to the contrary. The episode showed, in effect, that people enjoy the news that falls outside the margins of possibility and objectivity, preferring them to bland reports about science and politics. These arguably make everyday life more interesting in a gossipy way. The *Sun* ended publication on January 4, 1950, but it left a fake news legacy that has been taken up today by all kinds of tabloids and social media platforms. The lesson to be learned by the Great Moon Hoax is a concrete one: People tend to enjoy sensationalistic stories because they are surprising and

DOI: 10.4324/9781003349143-4

extraordinary. Some of the factors that make the current trends in fake news different from earlier forms are the increased sophistication employed in their production, with up-to-the-minute software and algorithms; the enormous scale on which fake news are now being produced; and the speed, efficacy, and range with which they are spread. Sometimes, however, what seems to be fake news may be only satire or parody, which uses misinformation on purpose to amuse users or to emphasize something, rather than to deceive. So, fake news may be distinguished not just by the nature of the falsity of its claims, but also by intent and by the audiences to which it is directed. Although false news have been concocted and spread throughout history, the term "fake news" was coined and diffused after the *Sun* moon story in the 1890s when similar sensational reports in newspapers became common—a type of journalism called, shortly thereafter, yellow.

For the present purposes, the focus is on the use of fake news as a political tool, which, like big lies and conspiracy theories, can sway minds. A robust example is the Russian-based interference campaign into the American 2016 presidential election, which disseminated seemingly legitimate information via social media channels to reinforce opinions and biases related to specific groups. The campaign was operated by a St. Petersburg company called the Internet Research Agency (IRA), which created fake social media accounts to impersonate American interest groups in order to spread disinformation. The IRA employed two main strategies. One was to dissuade African Americans from voting for Hillary Clinton, encouraging them to stay away from the voting booths. Another was to incentivize conservative voters to come out and vote for Donald Trump, who would clean up the political mess left by the Democrats and rectify the crooked politics that they had been carrying out behind the scenes—the cabal metaphor. As the Russian campaign showed, spreading fake information can have serious consequences, since it played on social discord in the United States, exacerbating it considerably—a discord that has not diminished. Once the mind switch has been turned on, it is almost impossible to switch it off.

Why would anyone genuinely believe fakery of this kind, even after it has been revealed to be false? The main reason seems to be that beliefs become so deeply embedded that it is hard to extricate them—the Da Vinci Code effect (Chapter 3). Another reason is that people need vindication of their beliefs, no matter what the truth of the matter might be, allowing them to think, literally, "you are the bad one, not me." The aim of this chapter is to decode the strategy of fake news in political lying and mind control, discussing how the same cognitive linguistic approach can be used in this area of political analysis. The objective is to show that the same metaphorical structures undergirding big lies and conspiracy theories are used to create fake news, rendering them more believable because of the displaced truth effect that such frames bring about—that is, the effect whereby the map is deflected to cover a false territory. This effect is in contrast with normal usage of language, whereby abstractions are framed through conceptual metaphors and metonyms in order to grasp the verifiable meaning of the territory. It becomes an interfering cognitive filter when the metaphorical map is used intentionally to mislead people for self-serving, opportunistic purposes. That is the ultimate objective of fake news.

Fake News

Simply defined, fake news is false or misleading information presented in the form of news—in newspapers, magazines, social media sites, and other media channels. It sometimes has the cynical aim of damaging the reputation of someone or something, including political opponents. An example emerged during the 2016 Republican primaries when Trump revived the JFK conspiratorial narratives to spread fake information which alleged that opponent Ted Cruz's father was with John F. Kennedy's assassin, Lee Harvey Oswald, shortly before he murdered the president, borrowing a *National Enquirer* story claiming that the father, Rafael Cruz, was pictured with Oswald handing out pro-Fidel Castro pamphlets in New Orleans in 1963. Trump put it as follows (cited in McCaskill 2016):

> His father was with Lee Harvey Oswald prior to Oswald's being, you know, shot. I mean, the whole thing is ridiculous, What is this, right prior to his being shot, and nobody even brings it up. They don't even talk about that. That was reported, and nobody talks about it. I mean, what was he doing—what was he doing with Lee Harvey Oswald shortly before the death? Before the shooting? It's horrible.

The strategy obviously worked, since Trump defeated Cruz in the primaries—it was not, of course, the only factor, but it cannot be excluded as having cast a conspiratorial light on Cruz, connecting him to one of America's most embedded of all conspiratorial frames—the JFK assassination.

Of course, falsehoods spread by gossip, big lies, and so on, have existed since the invention of the printing press and used by many to promote self-serving political causes. Already in the middle part of the eighteenth century, during the height of the Jacobite rebellion, populist printers in Great Britain put out fake news regularly, such as reports fallaciously claiming that King George II was ill, in an attempt to destabilize the status quo (Black 1987). This buildup of falsehoods started cascading into other channels of information, including reputable newspapers of the era, making it difficult for many to tell fact from falsity . But it was not until the subsequent century that this type of journalism became prominent as a popular and populist genre, spreading misinformation and disinformation through public channels . The power of fake news can be seen in how political autocrats and dictators have used it for attracting attention and for swaying minds, as was evident in Trump's fake JFK-related news directed at his rival, Ted Cruz. Two classic examples of how fake news have been used systematically by entire governments can be enlisted here—the Nazi press and the Soviet newspaper *Pravda*.

Shortly after rising to power in 1933, Hitler created the Reich Ministry of Public Enlightenment and Propaganda, headed by Joseph Goebbels—corresponding to

Orwell's Ministry of Truth. The Reich Ministry controlled the content of films, theater, music, the press, and radio broadcasts. In addition, Goebbels used the print and radio media to indoctrinate the German people with his own take on the news, filtering them to make them consistent with Nazi ideology. The *Völkischer Beobachter* ("People's Observer") became the official daily newspaper of the Nazis already in 1920. From the outset, it was obvious that journalists for the newspaper were grounding their stories on several central Nazi metaphors—including the cabal one whereby there existed a purported Jewish plan of world domination. In 1926, another Nazi newspaper, *Dir Angriff* ("The Attack"), further spread the antisemitic metaphor through its editorials, fake news, and conspiracy theories (Carey 2017). Especially prominent were animal-insect metaphors describing Jews (and foreigners) as "rats," "parasites," "vermin," "lice," "bacilli," and the like. These shaped the content of many fake news stories. The cabal metaphor was also incorporated to spread fake stories such as the takeover of banking by Jews in Germany or the deterioration of society because of liberal intellectuals who "spread their filth like a contagious disease."

Pravda became the official newspaper of the Communist Party of the Soviet Union, becoming a media organ of the Soviet Union's own Ministry of Truth, the Central Committee of the Communist Party of the Soviet Union. Other newspapers were founded as misinformation sources of other state bodies, but virtually all of them took their news feeds from *Pravda* (Roudakova 2017). It is no coincidence that the word *Pravda* means "truth." The newspaper continually put out fake news regarding the role of the West in world affairs, portraying it as "truth," using the same repertoire of metaphor frames of the Nazis, with headlines such as "rapacious sharks of imperialism" and "hydras of counter-revolutionism," along with the central metaphor of light and darkness, which was used to divide the world into "us" (bearers of the light) and "them" (harbingers of darkness).

Fake news has since become an international political tool for spreading false information with harmful intent, sometimes generated and propagated by hostile foreign actors, particularly during elections. The spread of fake news has increased with the rise of social media, at the same time that misinformation is seeping into the mainstream media, as political polarization, post-truth politics, and social media algorithms are now part of the universe of information. Significantly, a *BuzzFeed News* investigation found that fake news stories about the 2016 US presidential election received more attention and promotion on Facebook and other social platforms than top stories from major media outlets (Silverman 2016). It was during that election campaign that Trump coopted the term "fake news" for his self-serving purposes—both as a moniker to cast doubt upon credible news organizations that portrayed him in a negative light and as a tool against opponents, such as the fake news about Ted Cruz's father. He spread fakery constantly, using tabloid-style language such as "Kung flu" in reference to the coronavirus, an obvious allusion to the art of Kung Fu, associated with Chinese martial arts. With this frontpage type banner, Trump threw the blame for the coronavirus on China by allusion. This generated a whole slew of fake stories right after on social media, all of which revolved around anti-Chinese sentiment (Kurila 2021).

The use of fakery and headline-style populist language allow an autocrat to put the blame on others while deflecting it from himself, generating hatred upon them for the endemic ills that he himself has brought about. Orwell (1949: 186–187) saw this as the primary role of any totalitarian Ministry of Truth, which organizes information in such a way as to generate events such as what he called "Hate Week:"

> The weather was baking hot. In the labyrinthine Ministry the windowless, air-conditioned rooms kept their normal temperature, but outside the pavements scorched one's feet and the stench of the Tubes at the rush hours was a horror. The preparations for Hate Week were in full swing, and the staffs of all the Ministries were working overtime. Processions, meetings, military parades, lectures, waxworks, displays, film shows, telescreen programmes all had to be organized; stands had to be erected, effigies built, slogans coined, songs written, rumours circulated, photographs faked. Julia's unit in the Fiction Department had been taken off the production of novels and was rushing out a series of atrocity pamphlets.

As Harris (2011) has aptly put it, fakery works because "trust in government, corporations, and other public institutions has been undermined by lies." It has prolonged wars and even sparked them, such as the example of "false reports of weapons of mass destruction in Iraq [which] were both instances in which lying (at some level) led to armed conflict that might otherwise not have occurred. When the truth finally emerged, vast numbers of people grew more cynical about U.S. foreign policy—and many have come to doubt the legitimacy of any military intervention, whatever the stated motive." As a result, a cascade of countervailing fake news emerges making it virtually impossible to say anything of factual substance, "paralyzing doubts about even the most reputable sources of information" (Harris 2011). The likely reason for this is that it is "hard to abolish lies once they have escaped into the world: We seem to be predisposed to remember statements as true even after they have been disconfirmed" (Harris 2011). Harris (2011) concludes as follows:

> Lying is, almost by definition, a refusal to cooperate with others. It condenses a lack of trust and trustworthiness into a single act. It is both a failure of understanding and an unwillingness to be understood. To lie is to recoil from relationship. By lying, we deny others a view of the world as it is. Our dishonesty not only influences the choices they make, it often determines the choices they can make—and in ways we cannot always predict. Every lie is a direct assault upon the autonomy of those we lie to. And by lying to one person, we potentially spread falsehoods to many others—even to whole societies. We also

force upon ourselves subsequent choices—to maintain the deception or not—that can complicate our lives. In this way, every lie haunts our future.

Trump's constant attacks on liberal media as "enemies of the people" who spout "fake news" is a Ministry-of-Truth doublespeak projection strategy—blame your enemies for what you yourself do. On the other hand, Trump's praise of Fox News and supportive tabloid and alt-right social media was reminiscent of how dictators have always publicly proclaimed support for state-controlled journalism. Not only is his strategy consistent with totalitarian politics in general, but it is also consistent with a longstanding journalistic tradition in America that can be traced back to the advent of yellow journalism in the nineteenth century, as discussed above. It is not surprising that, like other autocrats, Trump has constantly called for government control and even censorship of what he labels as the fake news media. Perhaps he envisioned the Federal Communications Commission as his personal Ministry of Truth.

As in other areas of mind manipulation, Trump knew that his attacks on the media would be taken at face value by his supporters, given the deep state metaphor on which they were grounded. With the strategy of accusing the mainstream media as promoting fake news against him, he was thus able to frame the attacks on him as reinforcing the conspiracy theory that he was being victimized by the "enemy." From this whole situation, a media-based "fight for the truth" became an "information war" pitting styles of journalism against each other. Trump's accusations of the mainstream media for not supporting his immigration policies for example were coded statements related to the deep state notion:

> The Fake News is not mentioning the safety and security of our Country when talking about illegal immigration. Our immigration laws are the weakest and worst anywhere in the world, and the Dems will do anything not to change them & to obstruct-want open borders which means crime! (Tweet, June 20, 2018 at 7:25:17 AM)

One of Trump's most effective counter-strategies against legitimate criticism was to boast about himself, emphasizing how the "fake news media" downplayed his achievements via the deployment of strategic metaphorical discourse frames such as the following:

Statement: The Fake News Media is desperate to distract from the economy and record setting economic numbers and so they keep talking about the phony Russian Witch Hunt. (Tweet, June 4, 2018 at 3:41:55 PM)

Target: Trump's accomplishments

Metaphorical frame: the witch hunt (the investigation into Russian interference to support his presidential campaign) as an obstacle put in the path of his real accomplishments by the deep state and its media voice

Statement: So funny to watch the Fake News, especially NBC and CNN. They are fighting hard to downplay the deal with North Korea. 500 days ago they would have "begged" for this deal-looked like war would break out. Our Country's biggest enemy is the Fake News so easily promulgated by fools! (Tweet, June 13, 2018 at 8:30:49 AM)

Target: Trump's achievements as a deal-maker

Metaphorical frame: the mainstream (liberal) media are fighting a war against him to downplay his achievements

Statement: NBC NEWS is wrong again! They cite "sources" which are constantly wrong. Problem is, like so many others, the sources probably don't exist, they are fabricated, fiction! NBC, my former home with the Apprentice, is now as bad as Fake News CNN. Sad! (Tweet, May 4, 2018 at 5:45:31 AM)

Target: real truthful information

Metaphorical frame: information used against him is fake (a reversal projection strategy)

Statement: The Fake News Networks, those that knowingly have a sick and biased AGENDA, are worried about the competition and quality of Sinclair Broadcast. The "Fakers" at CNN, NBC, ABC & CBS have done so much dishonest reporting that they should only be allowed to get awards for fiction! (Tweet, April 3, 2018 at 5:34:18 AM)

Target: opposing media outlets

Metaphorical frame: traditional American view of competition is corrupted by the "fake news media"

As communications analyst Piero Polidoro (2018) has aptly observed, the rise and spread of the fake news counter-strategy did not occur in a void. It traces its roots to political, social, technological, and cultural forces that converged already in the nineteenth century, sparking a society-wide need to find quick answers to complex problems, as well as a distrust of the views of traditional authoritative institutions. This need and distrust have become evident today throughout cyberspace communications, where the tendency to accept information at face value, without critical interpretive filters, is now a habit of mind. Even those who do apply the filters are likely to be negatively influenced by the massive proliferation of actual fake news. We all have a saturation point after which we start to ignore the negative implications of fakery, having become mentally exhausted by the constant and continual dissemination of misinformation throughout the internet.

Aware of the power of Trump's metaphors, Lakoff came forward during Trump's presidency to examine the meaning of the word *fake* itself (in Northeast Arkansas

Community College Library 2022). To do so, Lakoff enlisted the example of the word *gun* as an analogy. Putting the adjective *black* in front of it (*black gun*) does not negate that it is a gun. It just specifies a certain quality of the gun, which still has the same primary function as any other gun—to shoot something. But the word *fake* is entirely different:

> A fake does not have the primary function, but is intended to deceive you into thinking that it does have that function, and hence to serve the secondary function. A fake gun won't shoot, but if you are deceived into thinking it is real, it can intimidate you.

The implication is that by putting modifiers in front of the word *news*—good, bad, unbiased, biased, liberal, conservative—the core meaning of *news* as information tethered to reality can be skewed. So, when Trump calls news *fake*, he transforms the meaning by a clever semantic trick—that is, he portrays the information as being untethered to reality. In other words, calling something fake news implies that it is not news at all. It is an Orwellian example of the Korzybski effect. As Lakoff goes on to say:

> It is done to serve interests at odds with the public good. It also undermines the credibility of real news sources, that is, the press. Therefore it makes it harder for the press to serve the public good by revealing truths. And it threatens democracy, which requires that the press function to reveal real truths. Calling real news fake is an attempt to hide the truth and undermine the function of the truth in a democracy.

Disinformation

Fake news come in two main forms: as misinformation, or false information spread unwittingly as assumed correct information,such as the genuine belief among some that vaccines are harmful, and as disinformation, which is false information spread intentionally, as for example, the blaming of racial groups for social ills.

The English word *disinformation* is a loan translation of the Russian term *dezinformatsiya*, coined by Joseph Stalin (Jowett and O'Donnell 2005: 21–23). Soviet planners in the 1950s defined it bluntly as the "dissemination (in the press, on the radio, etc.) of false reports intended to mislead public opinion." The tactic has been used throughout history, however, as a political and military ploy. A major strategy in disinformation discourse is what Steen (2015) calls "deliberate metaphorizing"—that is, the "intentional use of a metaphor as a metaphor." This consists primarily in making false data appear credible with metaphors such as "leading ideas," "solid facts," "stable opinions," and the like. The technique is effective because the fakers do not have to prove to anyone that their information is true in any empirical or demonstrable way. It just has to make sense, which is achieved via the utilization of a metaphorical strategy, which presents the falsehoods as if they were true.

Today, disinformation is spread mainly through the internet, intended to promote a particular political, social, or ideological agenda. It becomes believable to many because of its massive perpetration, whereby truth can become forgotten or ignored as a premise for honest communication. This was examined empirically in a 2016 research study of thousands of students ranging from middle school to college (Wineberg et al. 2016), which found that frequent online users were easily duped into believing disinformation if it occurs on social media sites used commonly by the users themselves. Many of the subjects were unable to distinguish fact-based news from their fake counterparts, regardless of their technical savvy. The conclusion of the study was a warning—fake news have become a facile way to activate the Da Vinci Code effect (as it has been called here). Free speech laws prevent the prosecution of the creators of fake content. For this reason, the issue of fake news has become a critical one in charting the future course of freedom of expression. Disinformation, clickbait, hoaxes, conspiracy theories, pseudoscience, and bogus content are so dominant today across social media that they induce an unreflective processing of information, rendering critical thinking immobile or unresponsive. It is the perfect cognitive environment for political manipulators to thrive in, since they can use it to "manufacture consent," to borrow a phrase from Chomsky and Herman (1988).

Significantly, Stalin founded a "Disinformation Office" in 1923—to produce fake news on a daily basis, a practice that has hardly evanesced in Russia under Vladimir Putin, who has used it to make Russian citizens believe that his invasion of Ukraine is necessary by spreading disinformation that the country was run by Nazis. Benito Mussolini also used disinformation tactics to rise to power in Italy in October of 1922, taking over the reins of the media to control the messages that they disseminated. He portrayed the government at the time as "a gathering of old fossils" (in Mussolini 2018), which became a constant metaphor in his messaging tactics, so as to persuade the youth of the era that his approach to governance was the path forward. As an editor for several newspapers himself, Mussolini had learned the art of message shaping firsthand, coming to use the press for his own ends. Shortly after his takeover of power, most of Italy's mainstream newspapers were suppressed, with a few smaller ones tolerated to convey the appearance that he supported freedom of the press. In Germany, Goebbels spread the same kind of disinformation, claiming that the Nazi government was working for the future of the youth of the country. This allowed Goebbels to recruit young zealots who displayed "ardor, enthusiasm, untarnished idealism" (cited in Irving 2018). Goebbels also took control of the pre-Nazi press, labeling Germany's newspapers at the time as "messengers of decay" that were injurious to the "beliefs, customs and national pride of good Germans" (Irving 2018). As a result, all journalism was subjected to *Gleichschaltung* (the standardization of political, economic, and social institutions in terms of Nazism)—implying that all journalists had to follow Nazi ideology on all issues.

The parallel uses of disinformation by political autocrats are remarkable. Today, there is actually no need for Disinformation Offices or Ministries of Truth—the main sources of disinformation are social media networks, whereby political manipulators can intervene personally to publish falsehoods broadly, so as to create confusion, one of the central aims of all Ministries of Disinformation of the past. It is little wonder, as Wheeler (2021) has aptly remarked, that Trump wanted the Federal Communications Commission (FCC) to control social media content, aware of the power of real, truthful information to influence opinions, claiming that it was liberals who used the networks to promote anti-American ideas, while conservatives were censored. Trump issued an Executive Order in which he complained that social media "platforms are engaging in selective censorship." He had clearly understood the power of social media in reaching young people. So, he also signed orders banning social media apps used commonly by young people, having become aware of the power of satirical humor used against him on the platforms to influence young people's minds. He justified the orders under the pretext that such media threatened the national security of the United States. Especially effective were videos ridiculing Trump's televised briefings on the coronavirus pandemic, garnering millions of views, portraying the president as a bungler intent on using any opportunity to aggrandize himself and to attack people outside his orbit.

The most salient example of the use of social media to spread disinformation is found in the so-called Russian Institute for Strategic Studies, which is pivotal to spreading falsehoods throughout the world. Putin used it, for example, to support Republicans and Donald Trump's 2016 presidential campaign. If Trump were to lose the election, then the Institute would shift its efforts to focus upon voter fraud so as to undermine the legitimacy of the electoral system and elections—a situation that actually crystallized after the 2020 election. Russia's disinformation tactics during the 2020 campaign included sending out insinuations about Democratic presidential candidate Joe Biden's mental fitness, amplified by Trump on Twitter.

The psychological mechanism required for disinformation to work is meta-phorical framing, since it can activate mind states automatically, as discussed throughout this book (the Korzybski and Da Vinci Code effects). As Lakoff (2003) has aptly observed, one cannot overemphasize the emotional power of using politically-motivated central metaphors to drive foreign policy and to shape opinions of the populace more generally—a fact corroborated by the use of this metaphorical strategy by Putin to justify his invasion of Ukraine. The main central metaphor was *a nation is a person,* which Putin used constantly, blaming different "persons" for the situation he himself created, claiming that the Russian people are ethnically and historically one and the same as Ukrainians. As Lakoff commented on the war against Iraq, which is applicable to the war in Ukraine: "They will kill many thousands of the people hidden by the metaphor, people that according to the metaphor we are not going to war against." Lakoff elaborates as follows:

> The Nation As Person metaphor is pervasive, powerful, and part of an elaborate metaphor system. It is part of an International Community metaphor, in which there are friendly nations, hostile nations, rogue states, and so on. This metaphor

comes with a notion of the national interest: Just as it is in the interest of a person to be healthy and strong, so it is in the interest of a Nation-Person to be economically healthy and militarily strong. That is what is meant by the "national interest."

As discussed in previous chapters, central metaphors become the basis for further metaphorizing, which carries forth the event structure of the initial overarching metaphor. In the case of the *nation is a person* metaphor the main derived subsidiary metaphor is what Lakoff calls the *rational actor* one, which encodes the concept that it is irrational to act against national interests. This is then used to justify "losses" including people maimed or killed in the conflict. As Lakoff puts it: "According to the Rational Actor Model, countries act naturally in their own best interests—preserving their assets, that is, their own populations, their infrastructure, their wealth, their weaponry, and so on." That is precisely what Putin claimed throughout his disinformation campaign to support his invasion of Ukraine. From these metaphorical frames, various other metaphorical concepts can be constructed, as well as conspiracy narratives, which Lakoff designates as the *self-defense* and *rescue* stories:

> In each story, there is a Hero, a Crime, a Victim, and a Villain. In the Self-Defense story, the Hero and the Victim are the same. In both stories, the Villain is inherently evil and irrational: The Hero can't reason with the Villain; he has to fight him and defeat him or kill him. In both, the victim must be innocent and beyond reproach. In both, there is an initial crime by the Villain, and the Hero balances the moral books by defeating him. If all the parties are Nation-Persons, then self-defense and rescue stories become forms of a just war for the Hero-Nation

If we substitute the name Putin for Hero, Ukrainian independence for Crime, Russia for Victim, and the West for Villain, we can easily discern how and why Putin's disinformation strategy resonated with many of his fellow citizens. As Lakoff concludes, the use of such disinformation metaphors cannot be ignored, since they affect the brain directly: "One of the fundamental findings of cognitive science is that people think in terms of frames and metaphors—conceptual structures like those we have been describing. The frames are in the synapses of our brains—physically present in the form of neural circuitry. When the facts don't fit the frames, the frames are kept and the facts ignored."

Pseudo-Events

In July of 1835, a grocer named Phineus Taylor Barnum came forward to announce publicly that he had purportedly purchased a 161-year-old slave named Joice Heth who, he claimed, had been George Washington's nanny (Reiss 1999). Barnum promoted his "purchase" as "Absolutely the greatest natural and national curiosity in the world." The ploy worked beyond his expectations—more than 10,000 people went to see Heth, who was an actual African American slave, at New York City's

Niblo's Garden during a two-week exhibition organized by Barnum. A poster created by Barnum, announcing the exhibition, is one of the first instances of bombastic metaphorical language that was to become typical in promotional, marketing, and political campaigns:

> Joice Heth is unquestionably the most astonishing and interesting curiosity in the World! She was the slave of Augustine Washington, (the father Gen. Washington,) and was the first person who put clothes on the unconscious infant, who, in after days, led our heroic fathers on to glory, to victory, and freedom. To use her own language when speaking of the illustrious Father of this Country, 'she raised him'. Joice Heth was born in the year 1674, and has, consequently, now arrived at the astonishing age of 161 years.

Eventually, Barnum admitted the hoax, but it did not matter, since people loved the idea, which, like the Great Moon Hoax, had become a form of entertaining news, no matter what the truth of the matter was. Even though the exhibition was a fake event, people loved it just the same, and many continued to believe it (or wanted to believe it) as truthful. In 1962, American historian Daniel Boorstin called such opportunistically-staged fake events, "pseudo-events," which he defined as events arranged merely for the sake of the publicity they generate, gaining plausibility because they are designed to appear spontaneous or unplanned.

The staging of pseudo-events has, since Barnum, become a major political strategy. As an example, consider Trump's staging on June 1, 2021, of a photo op at Lafayette Square in Washington holding a Bible, after protestors were cleared from the area—an action which showed how he could turn one event into another, namely a legitimate protest into a pseudo-religious performance. Trump knew clearly how to manufacture support through such performative pseudo-events, which also garnered him substantial media coverage. As Boorstin (1962: 207) put it:

> Our attitude toward our own culture has recently been characterized by two qualities, braggadocio and petulance. Braggadocio—empty boasting of American power, American virtue, American know-how—has dominated our foreign relations now for some decades. Here at home—within the family, so to speak— our attitude to our culture expresses a superficially different spirit, the spirit of petulance. Never before, perhaps, has a culture been so fragmented into groups, each full of its own virtue, each annoyed and irritated at the others.

Like Barnum, Trump had grasped intuitively that pseudo-events, like any form of spectacle, have great appeal, forming the basis for further fakery and subsequently-staged pseudo-events. As Boorstin (1962: 31) observed:

> Pseudo-events spawn other pseudo-events in geometric progression. This is partly because every kind of pseudo-event (being planned) tends to become

ritualized, with a protocol and a rigidity all its own. As each type of pseudo-event acquires this rigidity, pressures arise to produce other, derivative, forms of pseudo-event which are more fluid, more tantalizing, and more interestingly ambiguous.

Kevin Young (2017) has argued that both Barnum and Trump perpetrated hoaxes and pseudo-events because they lacked viable political ideas. Their intent was, as Boorstin noted, to engender a "national self-hypnosis," whereby fake and real events become indistinct. The origin of this psychological symptomatology can be traced, Boorstin suggests, to the late nineteenth and early twentieth centuries when Americans demanded new and exciting forms of entertainment and news at an unprecedented rate, much faster than they could possibly occur. So, Boorstin claims, the press and radio stepped in to fulfill this spreading desire, even creating news when none was available. The Great Moon Hoax may well be the first example of a news outlet satisfying this desire. The pseudo-event creates a sense of objective experience by simply providing the conditions to achieve the experience. Because of such unreal events, America entered into an "age of contrivance," in which illusions and fabrications superseded rational discourse and debate: "We suffer primarily not from our vices or our weaknesses, but from our illusions. We are haunted, not by reality, but by those images we have put in their place" (Boorstin: vii). Significantly, Boorstin alluded to *Mein Kampf,* differentiating pseudo-events from propagandistic information as follows (Boorstin 1962: 34):

> These pseudo-events which flood our consciousness must be distinguished from propaganda. The two do have some characteristics in common. But our peculiar problems come from the fact that pseudo-events are in some respects the opposite of the propaganda which rules totalitarian countries. Propaganda—as prescribed, say, by Hitler in Mein Kampf—is information intentionally biased. Its effect depends primarily on its emotional appeal. While a pseudo-event is an ambiguous truth, propaganda is an appealing falsehood. Pseudo-events thrive on our honest desire to be informed, to have "all the facts," and even to have more facts than there really are.

It can thus be inferred that it is through an amalgam of propagandistic lies and pseudo-events that the master political manipulator can bring about mind control. This can be seen saliently in Putin's overall Ukraine invasion strategy—in addition to the central metaphors used in his pronouncements, he staged a whole series of pseudo-events to create a state of national hypnosis, including a televised performance of solidarity with Ukrainian leaders that he himself had appointed to several regions after declaring the regions as part of the Russian Federation. These events were clearly designed to counteract the horrific images of human devastation in Ukraine that his war had brought about. As Boorstin (1962: 39) remarked: "Whenever in the public mind a pseudo-event competes for attention with a spontaneous event in the same field, the pseudo-event will tend to dominate. What happens on television will overshadow what happens off television."

Conspiracy theories, big lies, fake news, disinformation campaigns, and pseudo-events produce a simulacrum of reality, distorting it in ways that affect brain processes, likely rewiring the brain to accept falsehoods as a form of normalcy, indistinguishable from truth. They all have the effect of inducing people to put aside facts and focus on the pictures in the mind that disinformation generates, to cite Lippmann once again. Prefiguring the current era of international conflicts ignited by dictators such as Putin, Boorstin (1962: 261) issued the following warning:

> We must first awake before we can walk in the right direction. We must discover our illusions before we can even realize that we have been sleepwalking. The least and the most we can hope for is that each of us may penetrate the unknown jungle of images in which we live our daily lives. That we may discover anew where dreams end and where illusions begin. This is enough. Then we may know where we are, and each of us may decide for himself where he wants to go.

Epilogue

Information hoaxes actually have a long history, preceding the Great Moon Hoax episode. As far back as the 1270s BCE, Rameses the Great spread lies about the Battle of Kadesh, portraying it as a victory for the Egyptians, etching scenes of himself destroying his foes during the battle on the walls of his temples. The treaty between the Egyptians and the Hittites, however, reveals that the battle ended actually in a stalemate. Similar boastful stories aiming to manipulate the meaning of real events have marked the social and political landscape ever since. But never before the advent of the mass media, starting with the print medium, have hoaxes in the form of fake news and pseudo-events become routine, spreading broadly today through the internet. As Henry Giroux (2016) has observed, the fake news world in which we live is destructive of normal meaning expectations because it deeply alters people's understanding of facts and reality, obstructing the operation of normal cognitive processes to the point where the distinction between truth and lies is no longer seen to be relevant. The destruction of truth and its replacement by fakery has always been used by the political manipulators of history, including Trump:

> Trump's language attempts to infantilize, seduce and depoliticize the public through a stream of tweets, interviews and public pronouncements that disregard facts and the truth. Trump's more serious aim is to derail the architectural foundations of truth and evidence in order to construct a false reality and alternative political universe in which there are only competing fictions with the emotional appeal of shock theater.

Giroux's phrase "competing fictions" is a useful one. It describes how fake news, conspiracy theories, and big lies are just that—competing fictions, intended to sway minds away from objective truth. An example is in the area of climate change, which is a frightening reality that is now a real threat to survival, but dismissed as a hoax by conspiracy theorists, who construct fake scientific news to support their conspiracy, thus creating confusion, based on the related conspiracy theory that real science itself is part of the deep state. It is relevant to note that *The Oxford English Dictionary* identified "post-truth" as its 2016 word of the year, just before the US election, acknowledging the spread of fake news and disinformation through internet communications. In a post-truth world, false beliefs take precedence over logic, pseudo-science over real science, and apophenia over objective critical reasoning.

The deleterious cognitive effects associated with the contemporary era of fake news were eerily predicted by French social critic Jean Baudrillard (1983) with his notion of the simulacrum, or the idea that fiction and reality have become indistinguishable in modernity. Because of constant exposure to alternative facts, disinformation, pseudo-events, and conspiracies, the boundary between truth and falsehood has become a tenuous one. Baudrillard emphasized that the simulacrum emerges in four stages, which can be applied to the current era. First, there is the normal state of consciousness, inhering in a straightforward perception of reality and in a concrete awareness of the distinction between reality and fantasy. This is followed by a mind state that involves a perversion of reality produced by constant exposure to simulations and fictional portrayals; this is the stage in which alternative facts and conspiracy theories start to create doubt about reality. It then leads to the third state, when perception breaks down, incapable of filtering between what is real and what is false or just imaginary. The final stage is when the simulacrum becomes habitual, as people become more and more skeptical in accepting anything as true or even meaningful.

The Great Moon Hoax is an example of how the simulacrum is activated, playing on people's love of mystery and their fascination with unexplained phenomena, fueled by the cabal metaphor, or the belief that the government was hiding the truth about such things as extraterrestrial life. The articles claimed to show plants and other forms of organic life on the moon's surface. Many were dumbstruck by this image. Incredibly, the articles actually sparked debates on extraterrestrial life, outside of the scientific paradigm. The story had gained traction through the simulacrum, with new elements being added cumulatively to the plot line, evolving into what we now call a conspiracy theory. It is not clear if the fake information was a parody of science or a prank perpetrated by the editor, Richard Adams Locke, on a gullible readership, eager to read about conspiracies that tapped into an endemic distrust of the government and a thirst for stories of alien life. The moral is that we are all susceptible to the simulacrum if the story is unusual or extravagant, if the language is persuasive and immediate, and if we believe it is telling us something we suspect may be hidden from us.

5

MYTHIC LIES

Prologue

Hitler's central metaphor from which he concocted his pseudo-theory of racial superiority was based on a myth and thus on a form of unconscious metaphorical-narrative cognition that has deep historical-evolutionary roots in the psyche. Called the "Aryan myth," it is a classic example of what can be called a "mythic lie," or the fabrication of a mythological story to perpetrate a big lie, based on a central metaphor—the metaphor of a superior race. The myth actually emerged in the nineteenth century—an era in which scholars wanted to classify people of Indo-European heritage in terms of races (Dunlap 1944). As it has turned out archaeological evidence has never come forward to support the existence of a historical Aryan race. There was an Aryan dialect of an Indo-European language, but never a race as such. Its promulgation by the Nazis constituted a mythic form of history. In this case, the big lie was reformulated to activate mythological belief systems present in the unconscious part of the mind. A parallel mythic lie is the MAGA myth (discussed previously), whereby it is assumed that America was founded by a group of white colonists who were able to take over the land because of destiny.

Mythic histories are crucial to establishing distinctive cultural identities—hence their universal emergence across the ancient world. They become over time and constant usage, ritualized, symbolized, and, more crucially, accepted as founding stories, which describe the origins of shared values, worldviews, beliefs, and goals. Carl Jung (1959) referred to them as "archetypal stories," making them highly believable, even if they defy objective truth, because they are unconscious. These then become canonical metaphorical frames for justifying such actions as "war defenses," as Lenin proclaimed (Chapter 3), which often lead to disastrous consequences. Hitler's mythic story of an Aryan race of superior beings whose existence

DOI: 10.4324/9781003349143-5

was threatened by inferior beings brought about such consequences, including the Holocaust. As such, it is the classic example of how a made-up, but believable, story can instill hate into groupthink—a hatred of others who do not fit into the racial paradigm described by the myth and who are seen as upsetting the historical destiny of a people. Eradicating the "others" through any means thus becomes a rallying cry aimed at pursuing an overall false historical goal of world domination or, at the very least, of purification of otherness from a society. Once people insert themselves into the apocryphal storyline, they see themselves as valiant fighters in the ongoing outcomes of the mythic story, much like the mythic plots of ancient narratives, such as the Homeric ones. This makes it virtually impossible to cast doubt on the story's validity, given the high degree of emotional commitment made to it by individuals. Once drawn into it, escape from it is impossible for the simple reason that no one wants to admit to having believed a false myth.

As mentioned, Trump's MAGA narrative, which aims to depict an idyllic era of America, governed by white settlers with "real American values," which is being threatened by outsiders and by racial and cultural diversity from the inside, falls into this cognitive paradigm. It was intended to create belief in a cause by evoking pseudo-archetypal images of the past. Studying the conceptual structures of mythic speech involves examining the metaphorical frames that undergird it (for example, *racial purity is threatened by others*). A primary goal of this chapter is to discuss how such framing informs mythic speech and mythic thinking. For example, the MAGA myth is driven by the metaphor of *cultural purity*, which is *contaminated* by those who are not part of the real America. From this a *culture war* metaphor crystallizes that becomes embedded in groupthink, finding realizations and reifications in actual conflicts that America faced during and after the Trump presidency. False mythologies aim to present history as a linear process, whereby the past is seen as moving into the present, and must be preserved in its original forms, or else the past will be completely destroyed, as will the "real" culture of a society. False mythologies today are reinforced constantly because social media systems facilitate their communication, allowing people to share immediate feelings and reactions—a situation which has led to a "culture of instantaneity" that has put pressure on people to participate in ongoing falsehoods so as to be participants in a kind of communal mission to understand the world.

The ancient myths—stories of famines, floods, etc.—are stories that resonate to this day. Their power comes from recurring characters and plots that are based on understandable metaphorical themes (journeys, impediments, and so on). Even though we live in an age of science, mythic thinking as a mode of understanding has hardly disappeared. The French semiotician Roland Barthes cogently argued in his classic book, *Mythologies* (1957), that mythic cognition continues to be an unconscious factor in "naturalizing" beliefs. Modern-day myths are based on the same metaphorical structures as the ancient ones, but they crucially have different functions. The original myths emerged as a means to understand real events (before the advent of science). Today, the fabricated myths are intended to replace science

and objectivity. There is, of course, an instinctive sense of reality as it presents itself
to all humans, regardless of the language they speak or the images and symbols to
which they have been exposed. But this sense can be turned off or on by linguistic
and narrative manipulation, as discussed throughout this book. A mere word or
phrase, such as MAGA, can affect how people *think* about reality, given that it is
perceived to be coded with powerful historically-valid meaning, impelling believers
to accept its central metaphor of an *idyllic past* as being destroyed by those who are
not descendants of that past.

As Lakoff (2016b) has argued, the MAGA myth depends largely on the central
metaphor of *the strict father knows best* which then becomes the source domain for
derivative metaphors:

> In the strict father family, father knows best. He knows right from wrong and has
> the ultimate authority to make sure his children and his spouse do what he says,
> which is taken to be what is right. Many conservative spouses accept this
> worldview, uphold the father's authority, and are strict in those realms of family
> life that they are in charge of. When his children disobey, it is his moral duty to
> punish them painfully enough so that, to avoid punishment, they will obey him
> (do what is right) and not just do what feels good. Through physical discipline they
> are supposed to become disciplined, internally strong, and able to prosper in the
> external world. What if they don't prosper? That means they are not disciplined,
> and therefore cannot be moral, and so deserve their poverty. This reasoning shows
> up in conservative politics in which the poor are seen as lazy and undeserving, and
> the rich as deserving their wealth. Responsibility is thus taken to be personal
> responsibility not social responsibility. What you become is only up to you; society
> has nothing to do with it. You are responsible for yourself, not for others—who are
> responsible for themselves.

Lakoff used this metaphorical frame to explain why Trump became such a powerful
figure in America—a strict father figure with the moral strength to set things right
in the nation. As Barthes (1957: 148) cogently argued, this type of mythological
cognition is arguably the most powerful shaper of beliefs, actions, and even consciousness: "It takes hold of everything, all aspects of the law, of morality, of aesthetics, of diplomacy, of household equipment, of literature, of entertainment."

Mythologies

The term Aryan, as mentioned, was coined in the nineteenth century in reference
to a language spoken by people in the Indian subcontinent, whose origins are traced
as far back as 1500 BCE. It was writer Joseph Arthur de Gobineau (1856) who first
used the term "Aryan" to mean the "white race." This skewed view soon started to
resonate with false notions of a master race—a myth that gained traction in the first
decades of the twentieth century when the Nazi party came to power in Germany,

which twisted the meaning of the word Aryan to refer to a pure white race that was pre-destined to rule the world. That race was "chosen" (by biology and history) to lead the world; relegating other races to serving the master race or else becoming eliminated if they posed a threat. The metaphorical frame of being *chosen* is powerful because it has divine overtones, without naming the divinity. The Aryan myth simply mapped this source domain onto Nazi official history and policies, so as to allow the "master race" to finally rule the world and build a harmonious, orderly, and prosperous society. Many bought into this mythology. But the truth of the matter turned out to be just the opposite of what Hitler promised. His regime brought about terrorism, war, and the Holocaust, instead of harmony and prosperity.

Belief in racial superiority is not exclusive to a particular society or a specific era. It has existed since the dawn of history. Ironically, the ancient Romans saw the Germanic tribes as a race of barbarians that was barely human. This tendency to ascribe superiority to one's own people may go back to our tribal origins. Archeological evidence suggests that, as the early tribes became more culturally sophisticated around 10,000 years ago, seeking larger territories with more natural resources within which to live, they came to accept and accommodate, by necessity or coercion, members of other tribes within their broadening habitats. This led to what the anthropologist Desmond Morris (1969) calls the formation of super-tribes—expanded groupings of people that came together as a consequence of tribal expansion and tribal admixture, laying down the conditions for the emergence of the first civilizations. The problem is that the original "tribal instinct" was not eliminated as the super-tribes started becoming separate civilizations and entering into war with one another to assert their superiority.

Whatever the truth, the fact is that differences in genetic traits among different peoples (tribes) are quantitatively negligible. Geneticists have yet to turn up a single group of people that can be distinguished by their chromosomes (Sagan and Druyan 1992). There is no objective test that would allow us to differentiate the races on the basis of intellectual superiority, and therefore the supposed evidence that is brought forward is specious at best, and contrived at worst. So, from a purely biological standpoint, human beings defy classification into racial groups. Nevertheless, the historical record shows that from ancient times people have, for some reason or other, always felt it necessary to classify themselves in terms of such categories. It was the German scholar Johann Friedrich Blumenbach (1828) who put forth one of the first race-based systems of classification. After examining the skulls and comparing the physical characteristics of the different peoples of the world, Blumenbach concluded that humanity had five races: Caucasians (West Asians, north Africans, and Europeans except the Finns and the Saami), Mongolians (other Asian peoples, the Finns and the Saami, and the Inuit of America), Ethiopians (the people of Africa except those of the north), Americans (all aboriginal New World peoples except the Inuit), and Malayans (peoples of the Pacific islands). These five divisions remained the basis of most racial classifications well into the twentieth century and continue to be commonly accepted in popular thinking even today. But population scientists now recognize the indefiniteness and arbitrariness of any such demarcations. Indeed, many individuals can be classified into more than one race or into none. All that can be said here is that *race* may well be, in the end, a manufactured notion, not a biologically based one.

False mythologies such as the "master race" one, or other notions based on racial superiority or supremacy, persist nonetheless because of the power of mythic thinking, which can easily be manipulated by master liars to sow resentment and even hatred towards others. In attempting to bring society back to a supposed period of racial purity, mythic narratives such as the Aryan and MAGA ones, end up destroying society, by incentivizing people to rise up and literally take arms against targeted outliers. Mussolini used mythic thinking in his attempt to bring back the glory of Roman times to his society, by concocting a myth of Roman purity, ignoring that many Italians did not have such heritage. In a statement he wrote to commemorate the founding of Rome, on April 21, 1922, he made the following assertion, linking ancient Rome to Fascism (cited in Neocleous 1997: 25):

> Rome is our point of departure and of reference; it is our symbol, or if you like, it is our Myth. We dream of a Roman Italy, that is to say wise and strong, disciplined and imperial. Much of that which was the immortal spirit of Rome resurges in Fascism.

In Fascism, not only members of other races or ethnicities, but also "traitorous enemies from within" the superior race itself are seen as dangerous to the establishment of cultural purity. In the case of the French and Bolshevik revolutions, the inside enemies were members of the aristocracy; in the case of Fascism, Nazism, and MAGAism, the enemies were intellectuals and other elites who were chipping purportedly away at the true foundations of society with their effete ideas, such as racial and cultural inclusivity. To restore society to its real historical mission, the views of the liberal press and intellectuals must be attacked viciously through brutal slogans and clichés, as a means to retrieve the past by eliminating these inside enemies of history.

The Greeks separated types of speech and narrative forms into *mythos,* based on beliefs, and *lógos,* based on logic. The former term was coined by Aristotle to describe the language of tragedies, which were typically based on Greek mythology. *Lógos* was seen instead as the language of rational argumentation and science. It was also the language used in writing objective history, based on events and episodes assembled into a sequential story; mythic history, on the other hand, was episodic, not sequential, formulated in terms of events that are construed as immanent, that is, constantly operating at all times, and thus permanently pervading and sustaining original cultural paradigms. Historical narratives based on *lógos* are designed to provide a rational understanding of events; mythic narratives work instead on unconscious, latent forms of belief.

Most early myths had an important psycho-social function—they provided origin stories that allowed people to grasp the meaning of recurring themes in human life—good versus evil, life versus death, and so on. This type of language and thinking is powerful because it is perceived as unchangeable by time, and thus "true" in a metaphysical way. This is what makes a mythology such as the Aryan one effective in igniting false beliefs, since it cannot be challenged by historical facts and counter evidence. The deep state conspiracy narrative that American society has been destroyed by liberals and the spread of multicultural diversity works psychologically in the same way. It cannot be demonstrated as true or false in any objective way; it can only be believed in the same way that mythic stories are. As Orwell (1968: 6) so aptly put it, "Myths which are believed in tend to become real."

As Barthes (1957) cogently argued, the original myths have not disappeared; they are being constantly recycled. The former emerged as a means for people to understand real events, ascribing them to divine forces. They were *de facto* theories of the world, before *lógos* became prominent as a form of understanding. So, they invariably contain elements of truth, presented through *mythos*. The false myths that are imprinted in stories such as the Aryan and MAGA myths surface, instead, to provide explanations that fit in with hidden biases, prejudices, fears, or belief systems—they are hardly concocted to represent some element of objective truth. A false myth is a contrary-to-fact narrative and even a contrary-to-logic story that is almost impossible to eradicate because it literally "makes sense" on its own once it is accepted. To reiterate, the original myths reveal how early history was conceptualized. Homer's *Iliad* and *The Odyssey*, for example, recount events that corresponded to historical events via *mythos*, while Hesiod's *Theogony* provided a genealogy of the gods, furnishing insights into how the original myths emerged. In the fifth century BCE, the myths were presented in the new format of the theater, as can be seen in the tragedies of Aeschylus, Sophocles, and Euripides. It was, actually, in that era that the rejection of *mythos* began, as philosophers searched for more scientific explanations for the phenomena and events described in the origin stories.

But the penchant for mythic explanations has hardly disappeared and the reason for this is because it shapes unconscious thinking and beliefs via the power of *mythos* to generate its own models of reality. This might explain why the Aryan myth has never been eradicated from contemporary times, finding new life in neo-Nazi and white supremacy ideologies. The myth even allowed the Nazis to develop their own pseudo-scientific racial classifications in order to justify the genocide of groups of people which they deemed racially inferior. Hitler argued the case of Aryan superiority throughout *Mein Kampf* (1925). Below is just a sampling:

> All the human culture, all the results of art, science, and technology that we see before us today, are almost exclusively the product of the Aryan. If we were to divide mankind into three groups, the founders of culture, the bearers of culture, the destroyers of culture, only the Aryan could be considered as the representative of the first group. From him originate the foundations and walls of all human creation. Hence it is no accident that the first cultures arose in places where the Aryan, in his encounters with lower peoples, subjected them and bent them to

his will. As soon as the subjected people began to raise themselves up and probably approached the conqueror in language, the sharp dividing wall between master and servant fell. The Aryan gave up the purity of his blood, and lost his cultural capacity, until at last, not only mentally but also physically, he began to resemble the subjected aborigines more than his own ancestors.

This excerpt utilizes two main metaphorical frames: (1) *higher* meaning superior and *lower* meaning inferior, and (2) *purity* of blood. These are mapped against pseudo-racial categories. As Lakoff (1979: 203–204) emphasized, the danger in such mappings is that thoughts become real: "metaphors can be made real in less obvious ways as well, in physical symptoms, social institutions, social practices, laws, and even foreign policy and forms of discourse and of history." From the Aryan myth, two central metaphors were derived by the Nazis:

Frame: All those who are not of the good race are chaff. It is necessary for the members of the superior German race to care for the purity of their own blood, otherwise they will become extinct.

Source domain: blood

Target domain: racial purity

Intent: From the blood metaphor the Nazis twisted the notion of race into a self-serving biological predestination theory. Any non-Aryan blood type would defile the purity, which must be restored by any means possible.

Frame: Policies alone will not furnish the superior nation with the kind of moral armament that will enable it effectively to overcome the weaknesses and dangers from within the society. In order to elucidate this point of view Hitler referred to the supposed real origins and causes of the cultural evolution of mankind.

Source domain: obstacles to overcome

Target domain: moral superiority

Intent: Hitler argued that to *overcome* moral weaknesses the German nation must realize what its "real origins" are, allowing it to accept its own historically-destined moral superiority.

Lakoff (2022) has argued that all such metaphors are grounded in an overarching mapping system based in the central metaphor of war, which then becomes the rationalization for ensuing battles (cultural and military):

Hitler titled his autobiography Mein Kampf for a reason. In one word, he could crystallize his hate-filled ideological ramblings into a single, identifiable, and compelling concept: battle. Yet phrasing a political philosophy with the rhetoric of battle is not limited to the likes of Hitler. Politicians then and now, respected and unknown, American and foreign, have described their policies and visions in the vocabulary of war. The phrase "the War on [insert noun]" has become a crutch for U.S. politicians seeking support for their policies. In 1964, Lyndon Johnson declared a War on Poverty. In 1970, Richard Nixon declared a War on Crime. In 1971, he called for a "full-scale attack" to "conquer" the drug problem—and the media titled it the War on Drugs. In 2001, George W. Bush launched the War on Terror. These campaigns shape the lives of American citizens and the discourse in American media. Likewise, accusations that leaders and parties wage a War on Women, or a War on Jobs, or even a War on Christmas dominate partisan back-and-forth.

Alternative History

Alternative histories, as discussed, are powerful tools of mind control, especially since they cannot be falsified, being based on mythic thinking. As discussed above, they gain emotional power through the manipulation of the metaphors used to deliver them. Consider Trump's metaphor of the "Witch Hunt," as he has characterized investigations into his felonious activities. It is hardly just a figure of speech; rather, it is highly allusive, pointing to a tragic period of dangerous mind control in American history—the Salem witch trials in colonial Massachusetts in 1692–1693. These were persecutions rather than prosecutions. There is little doubt that Trump's opportunistic phrase is intended to evoke a sentiment of false persecution, undermining therefore the validity of any prosecution that ensues from any investigation, since it would be seen by believers as verifying the conspiracy against him by the deep state—itself the central metaphor influencing belief in the MAGA story.

Such narratives gain incremental credibility if they are repeated over and over, as they are, for example, through social media platforms. No countervailing argument can disassemble the narrative, in which the persecuted victim, Trump himself, is seen as a martyr at the hands of the forces of the deep state. It is the manipulation of *mythos* that is at play here; not *mythos* itself. The false story that America is being "invaded" by hordes of reckless and dangerous immigrants is another example of how Trump manipulates *mythos*. It is designed to evoke fears that those who come into a nation from outside are invaders and must be dealt with severely. As J. P. Linstroth (2018) has cogently observed, Trump tapped into a long-standing myth of nativism in America—namely that immigrants pose a threat to "native" American culture:

> Toward the end of the 19th-century and at the turn of the 20th-century, many in the US promoted "Nativism"—an all-white America where good jobs belonged to Whites, not foreigners. This was the historical period known as the "Second-Industrial Revolution," the "Gilded Age," and the "Progressive Era"—a time of enormous economic transformation for the country through industrialization and urbanization.

The real achievement of the Machiavellian liar is to get people to notice him as their only way out of their imagined dilemma. As in the ancient mythic stories, Trump emerged as a heroic figure in 2016 to set things right in the world, despite his flaws. The invasion myth allowed Trump to gain power over reality itself. To his followers, what Trump says is true, if *he* says it is. Trump is the only figure who appears distinct in the mind fog of history—everyone and everything else is a blur.

Alternative histories today have found fertile ground for dissemination, as mentioned, in cyberspace. The Web is now our mythic story-teller and the memetic maker of legends. As Richard Dawkins (1976), the originator of the term *meme* long before the internet, claimed, memes are as transferable as are genes. Whatever one might argue against this theory, one thing is for certain—as a metaphor of mind control via the internet the notion of meme works perfectly. Cyberspace and its meme structure might be changing—or mutating—human understanding, taking us back to a *mythos* form of consciousness where anything that appears in the medium of cyberspace, real or fake, is likely to be believed.

A main objective of alternative narratives is to "mobilize passions," as Robert Paxton points out in his 2004 book, *The Anatomy of Fascism*. The main passion mobilized through far-right social media platforms on a daily basis is a sense of overwhelming crisis, evoking the dread of the decline of morals and traditions brought about by the invasion of foreigners and the cultural destruction produced by multiculturalism. The invasion narrative allows the political manipulator to highlight his leadership instincts over those of weak citizens, who have fallen prey to the deep state views. Alternative histories reveal a form of Freudian projection that is self-serving, but ultimately destructive—blame others for our own ills.

Alternative historiography comes in two main forms—the partial or the total fabrication of history. The former involves the incorporation of actual events that are told in traditional histories into the reconstructed narrative, molding the real and the fictional into a storyline that taps into inherent beliefs about the past. Over time, this type of story starts to take on higher and higher degrees of verisimilitude, making it difficult to dispel it with counter-arguments and contrastive empirical evidence. The latter type inheres in a total fabrication of the past, constituting a false mythology. The classic case is, of course, the Aryan myth. It was obvious from the outset that this was false, as the linguist Max Müller wrote in 1888, stating that anyone who "speaks of Aryan race, Aryan blood, Aryan eyes, and hair, is a great sinner as a linguist" (Müller 1888: 120). Hitler adopted the Aryan myth nonetheless to perpetrate his imperialistic objectives, at the same time that he could use it as a racist justification for world domination by a "master race."

A likely reason why any kind of history can resonate as believable may well be found in the structure of historical narrativity itself. In effect, we are a historical species; that is to say, we evolve not only biologically, but also through the flow of historical events. We record our cultural evolution through narratives that create a sense of continuity from one era to the next and through which societies define themselves. Historical accounts start with foundation myths that are told to explain how we came into existence. Later societies produce stories of heroes and their legendary exploits. Examples include the story of Robin Hood in England who stole from the rich in order to give to the poor; William Tell in Switzerland who resisted tyranny and played a dominant role in Switzerland's liberation from Austria; Davy Crockett in America who died bravely in the battle of the Alamo in 1836 for Texan independence from Mexico. Britain, Switzerland, and the United States have made these heroes, and their stories, part of the foundational historical fabric of their societies. To this day, their stories are told in acknowledgment of their importance to society.

Psychologically, societies need to have a continuous record of important events and heroic figures that have made them distinct and meaningful. For this reason, there is an unconscious desire for them to be true in an objective sense—a desire that is manipulated by the clever construction of alternate histories. A made-up story such as the Aryan myth thus gains increasing believability as it spreads through the populace through repetitions in speeches, newspaper articles, radio, etc. It describes its own signifcant events and culture heroes. As the French writer Marcel Proust (1925) so aptly put it, "Time passes, and little by little everything that we have spoken in falsehood becomes true."

Central Metaphors

Recall Martin Luther King's masterful *I Have a Dream* speech (Chapter 2) and Lincoln's 1863 Gettysburg Address, both of which were effective because they revolved around a central governing metaphor (as discussed)—an image schema from which all other metaphorical images are derived. In the case of the King speech it was the dream metaphor, grounded in religious narrative implying an imaginary means to escape from slavery to freedom. Throughout the Bible, revelations come to prophets and holy people in the form of dreams. Lincoln's central metaphor was that of *rebirth*, as can be seen in the derived metaphors found throughout the speech:

> Our fathers *brought forth* ... a new nation ... *conceived* in liberty ... (but) any nation so *conceived* ... cannot long endure... *live* ... unless we the *living* ... resolve (to) have a *new birth*.

Central metaphors are found as well in the speeches, statements, and other kinds of texts of nefarious political actors, as discussed. In Hitler, it is the metaphor of racial superiority and in Trump of the deep state. The central metaphor imprints itself into the language of their speeches, converting it into self-sustaining textual-rhetorical structure, based on derivative metaphors. Consider the Aryan racial superiority metaphor as it manifests itself in Mein Kampf (1925):

> *Excerpt*: The struggle between the various species does not arise from a feeling of mutual antipathy but rather from hunger and love. In both cases Nature looks on

calmly and is even pleased with what happens. The struggle for the daily livelihood leaves behind in the ruck everything that is weak or diseased or wavering; while the fight of the male to possess the female gives to the strongest the right, or at least, the possibility to propagate its kind. And this struggle is a means of furthering the health and powers of resistance in the species. Thus it is one of the causes underlying the process of development towards a higher quality of being.

Derived source domains: struggle, ruck, disease, fight, health, possession, propagation, highness

Frame: The central metaphor of racial superiority suggests struggles to overcome lower forms of life which are "weak," "diseased, or "wavering," and the fact thay the male of the species "possesses" the female, given that he is stronger, and thus able to lead the way towards a "higher quality of being."

Excerpt: Aryan tribes, often almost ridiculously small in number, subjugated foreign peoples and, stimulated by the conditions of life which their new country offered them (fertility, the nature of the climate, etc.), and profiting also by the abundance of manual labour furnished them by the inferior race, they developed intellectual and organizing faculties which had hitherto been dormant in these conquering tribes. Within the course of a few thousand years, or even centuries, they gave life to cultures whose primitive traits completely corresponded to the character of the founders, though modified by adaptation to the peculiarities of the soil and the characteristics of the subjugated people.

Derived source domains: life, fertility, inferior, dormant, soil

Frame: In this case the central metaphor is mapped against life, fertility, soil, and other "natural" phenomena, implying that racial superiority is a part of biology, not a social construct.

Excerpt: Whenever Aryans have mingled their blood with that of an inferior race the result has been the downfall of the people who were the standard-bearers of a higher culture.

Derived source domains: blood, inferiority, higher

Frame: This excerpt makes it obvious that the central metaphor implies racial purity concretely, since mingling blood with an "inferior race" is the "downfall" of those who are the standard-bearers of a "higher culture."

As these excerpts show, the power of oratory depends on a central metaphor that imprints itself on the derived metaphors that deliver the message and intent of the oratory. In effect, the central metaphor is the hallmark of any effective political speech. It provides a conceptual core around which an argument can cohere, including a false argument.

While Trump's many metaphors might seem incoherent at first glance, they are actually grounded in the central governing metaphor of the deep state. Among the first to use this metaphor was *Breitbart News* in 2016, becoming a useful and opportunistic one for Trump during the presidential campaign and during his presidency. The deep state is based itself on the image schema of the "depth" of "political rot" below the surface of liberal government. It allows Trump to derive metaphors such as the "draining the swamp" one, since swamps are deep, dirty waters. This works as a connective strategy that makes seemingly disparate ideas coalesce into an overall understandable scenario of the plight of the world. It taps overall into a belief that liberalism and its elitist worldview has ensconced itself "deeply" into American politics and society at large and thus needs to be "drained," at the same time that it fits in with the conspiratorial narrative of persecution that Trump is spreading to protect himself—persecution from the political left. Trump has repeated these metaphorical frames so many times, in public and in social media, that they have become virtual habits of speech, activating both the Korzybski and Da Vinci Code effects.

The fact that we tend to believe such metaphors as *real* is indirect evidence that we do not perceive words as arbitrary signs, but rather as concealing messages about reality—that is, we tend to believe that the metaphors we hear and use enfold messages about the real world that require special interpretation. They are felt, to put it another way, to constitute miniature theories about the world. When metaphor is devised to conjure up false referents, a weird thing happens—we know they do not exist in reality but we still believe that they hide some truth, arguably because we feel that they contain messages that need to be decoded. There is no real thing called a *unicorn*. But the word still conjures up the image of a horse with a single straight horn jutting out from its forehead. We get this image from mythic stories, of course. But the fact that it pops up in the mind impels us to accept it as having some hidden significance, even though we know it is an imaginary referent. Actually, most of abstract language works this way—it produces a sense that the world can be codified and stored in the mind through words. In the hands of the master liar, language can be manipulated to evoke plausible worlds with no requirement to prove their validity or even existence.

So, a central metaphor such as the "deep state" one, which does not point to anything specifically, gains plausibility through allusion, repeated over and over. This type of verbal strategy is what makes it so dangerous: allies of the liar understand the coded allusive meanings and will even expand on them, manufacturing evidence for them, creating false narratives based on them, and so on.

Metaphorical artifice, in sum, impels people to perceive hidden connections among disparate referents in terms of a inherent connective code. For example, Trump often connects the deep state metaphor directly with the political left and the fake news media, suggesting at the same time that his rise to power made a dent in the supposed cabal, leading to significant accomplishments (jobs, the appointment of conservative justices, and so on):

"The Deep State and the Left, and their vehicle, the Fake News Media, are going Crazy—& they don't know what to do. The Economy is booming like never before, Jobs are at Historic Highs, soon TWO Supreme Court Justices & maybe Declassification to find Additional Corruption. Wow!" (Tweet, September 6, 2018, at 4:19 AM).

Needless to say, political actors do not use just one central metaphor, but may need more than one. Trump also used the "Wall" metaphor, to stop illegal immigrants coming in through the southern border of the US. The Wall is both a real structure and a metaphor, subtly allusive to historical walls built as a protection against invaders. As one of Trump's staunch supporters, Senator Lindsey Graham, bluntly admitted in late December of 2018, speaking to reporters in front of the White House: "The wall has become a metaphor for border security."

In the end, central metaphors, like the Aryan, deep state, and the Wall metaphors are "Just So Stories"—a term taken from *Just So Stories for Little Children* (1902) by Rudyard Kipling in which made-up stories are concocted to explain the origins of things. A "Just So story" is an artfully contrived metaphorical mythic story to support one's particular views, having no basis in fact.

Epilogue

As Lakoff (2016b) has so keenly observed, mythic lies need to be exposed for the benefit of everyone, otherwise, they lead to catastrophic events, such as the Holocaust and the invasion of Ukraine. He put it as follows:

> Certain things have not been allowed in public political discourse in the media. Reporters and commentators are supposed to stick to what is conscious and with literal meaning. But most real political discourse makes use of unconscious thought, which shapes conscious thought via unconscious framing and commonplace conceptual metaphors. It is crucial, for the history of the country and the world, as well as the planet, that all of this be made public.

The ancient myths are stories of the *Volk*, as Herder (1970) called them, stories that allow people to make meaningful connections among things for which they have no logical explanation, and thus to make sense of the world on the myth's own terms. A key lesson to be learned from Orwell's *Nineteen Eight-Four* is that it is easy to manipulate human minds—through clever and ingenious uses of mythic speech, because it resonates archetypally in the unconscious. It is in the restructuring of the myths to serve the political manipulator's current schemes and ends that they become dangerous.

Hitler and other dictators grasped the importance of constructing a mythic history for their heinous objectives, since it could persuade people of the importance of preserving their culture and presumed destiny as a society. This allows for "meaning control" by assigning to specific words and phrases in a mythic–narrative framework a sense and significance that plays on this inner need for historical validation. This type of strategically coded historiography is meant to tap into fears and resentments. The aim is to discard objective history and use the mythic lie to stoke embedded beliefs via derivative metaphorical slogans and symbols based on it—mirroring what the Ministry of Truth was appointed to do. As Orwell (1949) put it:

> Like an answer, the three slogans on the white face of the Ministry of Truth came back to him: war is peace, freedom is slavery, ignorance is strength. On coins, on stamps, on the covers of books, on banners, on posters, and on the wrappings of a cigarette Packet—everywhere. Always the eyes watching you and the voice enveloping you. Asleep or awake, working or eating, indoors or out of doors, in the bath or in bed—no escape. Nothing was your own except the few cubic centimetres inside your skull.

Central metaphors are so deeply embedded in the brain that we are hardly ever aware of their latent power to affect our thoughts and behaviors. When used in mythic-narrative frames, they allow the political manipulator to control the cognitive environment in a society so that his slogans can acquire legitimacy. The myth of a superior race can then be expanded in all kinds of directions, as we have seen in this chapter; whereby it gains cognitive strength by allowing people to extract their own meanings from it.

6

CHANNELS OF SPREAD

Prologue

A book published in 1900, titled *Fake News in Ancient Rome*, written by archeologist Nestor Marqués, provides one of the first historical accounts of how political lies and conspiracy theories were spread in ancient Rome before the advent of mass communications technologies. The main medium was gossip—spreading malicious rumors and calumnies at large gatherings, which were then reinforced and spread via further gossip throughout Roman society. But close behind this oral medium for spreading falsehoods was the literary one. As Marqués claims, Virgil's *Aeneid*, apart from its indisputable literary value, was "a work commissioned by Augustus to convince the people of Rome to surrender their power, because it would be in their best interest." False news were also spread by posters and an early newspaper founded by Julius Caesar in 59 BCE, called *Acta Diurna* ("Events of the Day").

From the beginning of recorded history, it has become saliently obvious that for big lies and conspiracy theories to penetrate groupthink, they require channels of dissemination for communicating, transmitting, and reinforcing them repeatedly. With the advent of mass electronic media in the early twentieth century, the reach of politically motivated lies expanded dramatically, arguably changing the world of politics drastically. A classic early example of the use of the cinematic medium for this purpose is D. W. Griffith's *The Birth of a Nation* (1915). At one level, the movie deals simply with the purported history of the Civil War and the rise of the Ku Klux Klan. But inherent in its thematic subtext is the idea that the Klan was instrumental in shaping the foundations of America—a theory that has not escaped modern-day white supremacists. Aware of what he had done, Griffith designed his subsequent film, *Intolerance* (1916), to attenuate the effects of his previous movie, but it may have been too late, since the ideas in *Birth of a Nation* are now common among many hate groups.

DOI: 10.4324/9781003349143-6

The main channel of spread today is the internet, where conspiracy theories, fake news, and the like are often born and spread globally. This chapter will look at channels of spread as intrinsic to the perpetration and perpetuation of big lies and conspiratorial narratives. Humans have an instinctive tendency to think and act like the majority in their group—and it is this tendency that may be at the source of why big lies and conspiracy theories are so successful as they spread throughout internet forms of communications. As social beings, we are inclined to follow leaders and accept the beliefs of others in order to fit in. A dramatic example of this was the Russian hacking of the 2016 American election, mentioned several times, which is attributed to this phenomenon—that is, people started assuming that what others believed about a politician was important and true, thus becoming convinced to vote for the politician that the hackers had surreptitiously presented as the only real choice to "save America." As British philosopher Bertrand Russell (1950) eloquently remarked before the advent of the digital universe: "Collective fear stimulates herd instinct, and tends to produce ferocity toward those who are not regarded as members of the herd." Although lobbyists and other kinds of influencers existed before the internet, the social media universe has given voice to groups, such as QAnon, whose sole reason to exist is to promote political lies and conspiracy theories. To quote Hannah Arendt (1978): "A people that no longer can believe anything cannot make up its mind. It is deprived not only of its capacity to act but also of its capacity to think and judge. And with such a people you can then do what you please."

The Spoken and Written Word

In Greek mythology, the god Dolos ("Deception") was renowned for his mendacity, trickery, guile, and all the other tactics that are deployed by the consummate deceiver. Among his devious actions was his fake copy of the statue of Aletheia, the goddess of truth, which he created to deceive people into believing that they were looking at the real statue—trying to show how truth is an unreliable concept. The statue even duped Prometheus, who was struck by its similarity to the real statue. The story of Dolos is a cautionary tale. The Greeks recognized that liars have the ability to rise up above everyone else and gain their attention through their deceptions and trickeries. They often become larger-than-life figures who are admired, feared, and hated all at once. At the same time, they might unwittingly engender a process of social self-analysis, allowing people to think seriously about truth, history, and the future. The myth of Odysseus falls into this category. As King of Ithaca and central figure of the Homeric epic, *The Odyssey*, Odysseus was a master liar who, as if driven to do so by some inner compulsion, tried to deceive anyone who came into his sphere, including his wife, Penelope. For Odysseus, to speak meant to lie. Strangely, we take pleasure to this day in reading about Odysseus' exploits, admiring his mendacity as a manifestation of ingenuity and cleverness. We do not see his mendacity as something that is necessarily immoral, but as an intrinsic part of how a powerful person conducts his affairs.

Odysseus uses deception successfully to ultimately defeat the Cyclops, who is much bigger and stronger than he is and a much greater danger to the world.

Myths were transmitted orally, by and large. Many lies were spread through the spoken word—so much so that some, like Athenian historian Thucydides, issued a caveat regarding the persuasive nature of oral mythology. Thucydides viewed the political behavior of individuals and the subsequent outcomes of relations between states as ultimately mediated by fear and self-interest—hence the use of mendacity as a political weapon, a way of creating alternate truth so as to dupe people into seeing what is not there. The political liar is a master illusionist, Thucydides suggested, using techniques that hide his true intents and which he uses to control his victims, simply by being able to control oratory on his own terms.

The counter-weapon to political manipulation was comedy. Aristophanes' play *The Babylonians* was denounced by Cleon, the Athenian general and politician because he was portrayed in a negative, merciless way as a liar and champion of demagogic politics. What Aristophanes seems to have sensed is that such a politician appealed on some unconscious level to average citizens, who voted enthusiastically again and again to support Cleon, a grifter who did nothing but ruin and steal from those who backed him. Cleon's power of persuasion lay in his forceful anti-intellectual style of oratory during campaigns. Projecting forward to the American 2016 presidential campaign, we can see how portentous Aristophanes' message was. Hillary Clinton's campaign slogan of "Ready For Her" was static, specific, and exclusive, falling outside the powerful suggestive ambiguity of the MAGA slogan used by Trump, which became a metaphor for a cultural movement. Like Cleon, Trump used a profane style of oratory, which made him a kind of anti-hero who would smash all the elitist norms of the Clinton and Obama regimes. As Clifton (2017) has pointed out, the parallels between Cleon and Trump are striking:

Donald Trump is nothing new. His ilk have been around since the inception of democracy, and since then they have wrought havoc on democratic societies. Our ancient forebears have warned us about them in no uncertain terms. When the demagogue Cleon rose to power in Athens, the cradle of Western democracy, the ancient sources were explicit about the danger he posed, testifying to future generations of the necessity of opposing such figures. And yet, Cleon rises again and again to terrorize democratic societies.

Clifton goes on to warn that Athens never regained the power it once held, surpassed by Sparta and Thebes. Athenian democracy returned, but "the damage to Athenian power had already been done. Like the rest of the city-states, weakened by almost constant warring, Athens finally lost the independence it had enjoyed since its foundation to the conquering armies of Macedon." Political campaigns have always provided the contexts in which political schemers could get their messages across effectively, especially at rallies and other speech-based events. The great liars have always been great persuasive orators and performers, like Cleon.

Hitler, for example, always arrived late at rallies, which helped to develop tension and a sense of expectation in the crowd. When he took the stage, he stood to attention and waited until there was complete silence before starting to speak, ranting and raving about the injustices done to Germany, playing on the audience's emotions. By the end, the audience would be in a state of near hysteria. As soon as his speech was finished, Hitler would quickly leave the stage and disappear from view. Virtually the exact same performance script was deployed by Trump at his rallies. As Hitler knew (from *Mein Kampf*): "I know that men are won over less by the written than by the spoken word, that every great movement on this earth owes its growth to orators and not to great writers."

It is little wonder that Hitler went on to analyze why oratory works, as a way of preying on the gullibility of the masses, as he emphasized (from *Mein Kampf*):

All propaganda must be popular and its intellectual level must be adjusted to the most limited intelligence among those it is addressed to. Consequently, the greater the mass it is intended to reach, the lower its purely intellectual level will have to be. But if, as in propaganda for sticking out a war, the aim is to influence a whole people, we must avoid excessive intellectual demands on our public, and too much caution cannot be exerted in this direction. The more modest its intellectual ballast, the more exclusively it takes into consideration the emotions of the masses, the more effective it will be. And this is the best proof of the soundness or unsoundness of a propaganda campaign, and not success in pleasing a few scholars or young aesthetes. The art of propaganda lies in understanding the emotional ideas of the great masses and finding, through a psychologically correct form, the way to the attention and thence to the heart of the broad masses. The fact that our bright boys do not understand this merely shows how mentally lazy and conceited they are.

While oratory has always been a powerful medium for political schemers to prey on people's minds, the written word has also been coopted by them opportunistically. For example, in the years preceding the French Revolution, myriad pamphlets appeared in cities and towns throughout France, reporting details of the government's spectacular budget deficit. Each type of pamphlet came from a separate political camp, and each contradicted the other with different facts. Eventually, through government leaks and verifiable accounts, enough information was made public for readers to glean a general sense of the state's finances; but, like today, readers had to be both skeptical and willing to figure out the truth—a situation to which Socrates paid constant attention. Socrates taught that everyone is born with the ability to figure things out by reasoning about them. As Plato recounts in his text *Meno* (2019), Socrates even led an unschooled individual to grasp geometrical ideas by getting him to reflect upon them systematically. However, Socrates also knew that the same type of reasoning can be used to deceive or even harm someone. As he remarked, "False words are not only evil in themselves, but they infect the soul with evil."

As an example of how false words can affect us psychologically and even physically, consider the argument made by Susan Sontag in her 1978 book, *Illness as Metaphor,* in which she claims that some metaphors can be dangerous, literally, affecting people's health, since they have moral judgments built into them, which can become psychosomatic triggers that affect not only how we think about an illness, but also how we might react to it physically. Using the example of cancer, Sontag suggested that in the not-too-distant past the very word *cancer* would have been more deleterious to a patient's health than some of the actual physiological aspects of the malignancy from which they suffered: "As long as a particular disease is treated as an evil, invincible predator, not just a disease, most people with cancer will indeed be demoralized by learning what disease they have" (Sontag 1978: 7). Common examples of how we refer to cancer to this day bring out the validity of Sontag's main argument:

Cancer is a *killer.*
Cancer is a *predator.*
It's an uphill *battle* to beat cancer.
Cancer is a *scourge.*

These metaphors instill the unconscious perception that cancer is an "enemy" which must be defeated, rather than a clinical condition. The most dangerous metaphors, however, are those that depict cancer as a metaphysical force that has attacked someone for moral (or immoral) reasons ("She had it coming with her smoking habits;" "What did he do to bring about his cancer?" etc.). Sontag's point that people suffer as much from the metaphors about their disease than from the disease itself is, indeed, a well-taken and instructive one. A decade after *Illness as Metaphor,* Sontag wrote a similar treatise on AIDS (Sontag 1989), finding a similar pattern with regard to that disease—namely as punishment for a lifestyle choice. Once bodies and diseases are metaphorized, they seem to act upon real bodies. It is remarkable, as Mussolf has perceptively written, that the same kind of "body metaphors" were used by Hitler for his racist agenda of extermination of Jews (Mussolf 2007):

Applying methods of cognitive metaphor analysis to Hitler's antisemitic imagery in Mein *Kampf,* especially to the conceptualization of the German nation as a (human) body that had to be cured from a deadly disease caused by Jewish parasites [reveals] the conceptual domains of biological and medical categories form a partly narrative, partly inferential-argumentative source 'scenario', which centred on a notion of blood poisoning that was understood in three ways: a) as a supposedly real act of blood defilement; b) as a part of the source scenario of illness-cure; and c) as an allegorical element of an apocalyptic narrative of a devilish conspiracy against the 'grand design of the creator'. The conceptual differences of source and target levels were thus short-circuited to form a belief-system that was no longer open to criticism. The results cast new light on central topics of Holocaust research, such as the debates between more 'intentionalist' and more 'functionalist' explanations of the origins of the Holocaust, and the question of how the Nazi metaphor system helped gradually to 'initiate' wider parts of the German populace into the implications of the illness-cure scenario as a blueprint for genocide. The Nazi antisemitic metaphor system thus provides a unique example of the cognitive forces that can be unleashed in the service of racist stigmatization and dehumanization.

By creating lies so outrageous that they will be believed, Hitler claimed that they would literally debilitate people (from *Mein Kampf*):

All this was inspired by the principle—which is quite true within itself—that in the big lie there is always a certain force of credibility; because the broad masses of a nation are always more easily corrupted in the deeper strata of their emotional nature than consciously or voluntarily; and thus in the primitive simplicity of their minds they more readily fall victims to the big lie than the small lie, since they themselves often tell small lies in little matters but would be ashamed to resort to large-scale falsehoods. It would never come into their heads to fabricate colossal untruths, and they would not believe others could have the impudence to distort the truth so infamously. Even though the facts which prove this to be so may be brought clearly to their minds, they will still doubt and waver and will continue to think there may be some other explanation. For the grossly impudent lie always leaves traces behind it, even after it has been nailed down, a fact which is known to all expert liars in this world and to all who conspire together in the art of lying.

Hitler was also aware that the written word was also powerful in shaping minds—hence his control over print media and the identification of books permitted (or not) in Nazi society. On May 10, 1933 the Nazis mobilized student groups at universities across Germany to carry out a series of book burnings of works that were characterized as bearing an "un-German spirit." Enthusiastic crowds witnessed the burning of books by intellectuals, scientists, and cultural figures, many of whom were Jewish. Ironically, among the books thrown into the flames were those of the nineteenth century Jewish poet Heinrich Heine, who in his 1821 play, *Almansor,* had penned the ominous prophetic words: "Where they burn books, they will, in the end, burn human beings too." The Nazis were also aware of how to use the written words of the "enemies of the people" against them by dissimulation. The one that served these purposes best was *The Protocols of the Elders of Zion* (mentioned briefly in Chapter 1). The text was first published in Russia in 1903, translated into multiple languages, and disseminated internationally in the early part of the twentieth century, playing a key part in popularizing belief in an international Jewish conspiracy. Annotated versions of the work were assigned by some German teachers to schoolchildren after the Nazis came to power in 1933, despite having been exposed as fraudulent by the British newspaper *The Times* in 1921 and the German *Frankfurter Zeitung* in 1924. Allegedly constituting the minutes from meetings of Jewish leaders, revealing their "secret plans" to rule the world by manipulating economies, controlling the media, and fostering religious conflicts, the Nazis could claim that their anitsemitic warnings were not imaginary, but documented in the (false) text.

As the foregoing discussion was meant to illustrate, controlling the spoken and the written word has always been part of the strategies of political autocrats. Today, the channel to which they turn the most is the digital one, given its reach and ability to conceal the truth via memetic fragmentations of the mendacious message, which create the illusion of truth inherent in the fragments. All one has to do is connect the fragments into a believable conspiratorial story. Marshall McLuhan's (1964) term "global village" designating a world that depends upon electronic media for information and is thus united, electronically, as if in a "village", is an apt one. In the 1960s McLuhan predicted that electronic media would have an impact far greater than that of the content they communicated. He argued that this is so because the medium in which information is recorded and transmitted is decisive in determining the cognitive character of a culture: for example, an oral tribal culture is different from a writing-based one, because it perceives its history and truth exclusively through the subjective interpretations of the story-teller; while an alphabetic culture, which uses the written word to record its history, envisions itself as based on a more objective view, which it can transmit via the written word to others outside of the tribe. Literacy is thus what made early non-tribal collaborations possible. This was expanded by the advent of an electronic culture, McLuhan claimed, because people the world over can see themselves as participants in events going on in some other part of the world by simply switching on their television sets, and today by going online, as if living in a virtual global village. As he put it in 1962: "The human family now exists under conditions of a global village. We live in a single constricted space resonant with tribal drums."

Alongside his widely known catchphrase, "the medium is the message," McLuhan's characterization of the modern world of electronic mass communications as a global village captures perfectly the kind of consciousness we have all developed by living in electronically mediated mind space, whereby we all feel connected to each other anywhere on earth—at least potentially—through our electronic-digital tools. McLuhan claimed that the media in which information is recorded and transmitted are decisive in shaping trends and in charting future progress, since they extend human faculties (biological, mental, institutional) significantly, re-calibrating the senses and, thus, leading to a rewiring of the brain. The communication environment in which we interact, create, and express ourselves is no longer just real space, but also an electronic space where sensory modalities are becoming more and more part of a simulacrum. In this space, the mind is exposed to subtle manipulation, because it tends not to filter the information, but to simply accept it as it presents itself. The unexpected and unpredictable rise of Donald Trump as a Republican president was bolstered by the lowering of this critical filter. The hacking of the election played on resentments brewing in America between far-right conservative beliefs and the liberal practices that characterized the Obama administration. The ads used in the hacking undoubtedly affected minds, lowering the cognitive filter that detects falsehoods . When challenged that they might have been duped by the disinformation, causing cognitive dissonance, people tend to reject the relevant counter-evidence. After the election, several TV news organizations interviewed Trump supporters, challenging them with the "fact" that they were influenced by the hacking. It comes as no surprise that most of them rejected the challenge, saying that the information was true. Others admitted that it may have been false, but that it still "told it like it is." To quote McLuhan one more time: "Man in the electronic age has no possible environment except the globe and no possible occupation except information-gathering" (McLuhan 1998: 27).

Social Media

Recognizing the power of social media to sway people's minds, right after his invasion of Ukraine in February of 2022, Russian president Vladimir Putin, recalling Nazi Germany, instantly put state controls over both traditional and social media throughout the country. Using a form of Freudian projection cleverly, Putin then signed a new law that threatened up to 15 years in jail for Russians who posted "fake news" about the invasion. As in other dictatorships, Putin's shutdown of media platforms was intended to stem free political speech in Russia. And even though Russians could find other sources, such as Telegram, it was by shutting down major platforms that Russians became isolated communicatively with each other and the rest of the world. The paradox is that the same media are used by liars and truth-seekers alike, creating veritable virtual tribes fighting each other over the control of meaning.

One of the most dramatic examples of how social media can be used for strictly political and paramilitary purposes, was their use to plan, coordinate, and carry out the January 6, 2021 attack on the US Capitol by extremist groups, spearheaded by Donald Trump's verbal clarion calls. Platforms such as Telegram, Parler, and Gab were used before and throughout the 2021 storming of the Capitol, as members within the groups shared tips on how to avoid law enforcement and what their plans were with regards to carrying out their objectives. It should come as little surprise to find that QAnon played a major role in the insurrection, providing Trump loyalists with justifications for the insurrection, spinning conspiracy theories supporting Trump's big lie. QAnon opportunistically used a central governing metaphor to further incite the insurrectionists—the Great Awakening one, which inundated the social media airwaves before, during, and after the insurrection:

Source: The Great Awakening refers to a number of periods of religious revival American Christian history, characterized by waves of increased religious enthusiasm. Each Great Awakening was characterized by widespread revivals led by evangelical Protestant ministers, followed by a sharp increase of interest in religion, a profound sense of conviction and redemption on the part of those affected, and the formation of new religious movements and denominations.

QAnon metaphor: QAnon adapted this notion to its overall narrative related to the role of Trump as the "chosen one" for bringing about the new Great Awakening, leading people into a new era of Christian religiosity, which will have to be ascertained by revolutions and armed conflict—hence the motivation and rationale for the January 6 insurrection.

Source: The Storm—a metaphor that spans an infinite domain of notions (as discussed previously)—is what some Great Awakenings bring about.

QAnon metaphor: QAnon operates under the assumption that a national war between good versus evil is being concealed from public knowledge. The Storm refers to excessive social conflict that is predicted to occur prior to society reaching the point of "The Great Awakening".

As Jack Braitich (2021) has remarked, QAnon has developed a national social network for promoting a pseudo-holy war through social media, amplified by a president who is believed to have been sent to Earth to bring about the Great Awakening. To believe QAnon requires rejecting traditional political institutions, ignoring objective facts, battling apostates, and despising the mainstream press. One of Q's constant rallying cries is "Enjoy the show," a phrase that is interpreted as a reference to a coming apocalypse, when QAnon members will be spectators to the battle between good and evil (LaFrance 2020).

In 2020, as the QAnon movement became an international phenomenon, Pizzagate (Chapter 3) gained new traction and became global, with videos and posts on the conspiracy in other countries. The new iterations were less partisan and even ambiguous, indicating how different meaning is extracted from the same central metaphor. The majority of the promoters of the #PizzaGate hashtag were on TikTok and were mainly adolescents who were not necessarily sympathizers of right-wing politics, but may have even supported liberal causes. The idea of conspiracy thinking itself is what seems to attract virtually everyone in the global village, where a general Da Vinci Code effect seems to be coagulating. For example, singer Justin Bieber's 2020 song "Yummy" was alleged to be about the Pizzagate conspiracy theory, gaining traction after a Venezuelan YouTuber made a video about Bieber's song and its alleged references to Pizzagate, becoming a trending meme on the Spanish-language Twitter network. There is no indication whatsoever that Bieber had any political intentions with his song . He may well have been a victim himself of the Da Vinci Code effect.

Social media platforms constitute the most effective communicative channel for a lie to spread and become perceived as truth. It is the medium where information is "shared," not "reported," so that it is perceived as more reliable. The information is thus curated in ways that makes it more likely to fit a user's worldview. Social media thus allow the conspiracist to present the world to specific audiences in the way they would like it to be rather than how the world actually is. As Ryan M. Milner (2016) has cogently argued, it is almost impossible to imagine a major cultural or political moment that does not produce a constellation of hashtags, videos, and memes that comment on it via limitless iterations. The problem is that the virtual environment in which these emerge and spread inhibits the ability to filter out those that are patently fake, fraudulent, or conspiratorial. Needless to say, many hashtags and memes have been used as well to espouse some social justice cause. A perfect example is the #MeToo hashtag campaign in which actress Alyssa Milano encouraged survivors of sexual abuse to post "#MeToo" to raise awareness—a meme that clearly reverberated intertextually with other memes and texts designed to highlight social justice issues. However, this social media campaign resonated primarily with those already predisposed to espouse social justice issues; social media platforms with a contrary view actually used it as fodder for reinforcing counter-conspiracies.

Above all else, the cabal metaphor is what drives the enthusiasm of followers. QAnon's #ReleaseTheMemo campaign, for instance, which pushed for the release of an intelligence memorandum purportedly detailing missing FBI text messages to "imaginary secret societies plotting internal coups against the president" saw an enormous increase in tweets with the same hashtag immediately thereafter. The message had turned on the Da Vinci Code switch. And when that happens it is almost impossible to switch it back off.

Epilogue

McLuhan foresaw danger in the enthusiasm over new media (McLuhan 1964). He warned that they might make us mere "spectators," inclined to abrogate our responsibility to think and act independently, thus debilitating true democracy and its ontological foundations on critical debate. In a similar vein linguist and political theorist, Noam Chomsky (2002: 16), referring to Walter Lippmann, made the following relevant observation:

Now there are two "functions" in a democracy: The specialized class, the responsible men, carry out the executive function, which means they do the thinking and planning and understand the common interests. Then, there is the bewildered herd, and they have a function in democracy too. Their function in a democracy, Lippmann said, is to be "spectators," not participants in action. But they have more of a function than that, because it's a democracy. Occasionally they are allowed to lend their weight to one or another member of the specialized class. In other words, they're allowed to say, "We want you to be our leader." That's because it's a democracy and not a totalitarian state. That's called an election. But once they've lent their weight to one or another member of the specialized class they're supposed to sink back and become spectators of action, but not participants.

The success of a big lie has always depended on how it gains traction through diffusion. At no other time in history has this diffusion become so massive as it has in today's social media universe. To cite Richard Wooley (2018), social media have provided a fertile ground for the "illusion of knowledge:"

> Trump's specious solutions to the economic and security challenges facing the United States may resonate with people who can't explain or comprehend why they are suffering and why no help has come along yet. His ideas channel confusion and anger into comfortable solutions.

As Aldous Huxley (1934: 12) also wrote, in-group savvy is a powerful motivating force in human behavior: "To associate with other like-minded people in small, purposeful groups is for the great majority of men and women a source of profound psychological satisfaction. Exclusiveness will add to the pleasure of being several, but at one; and secrecy will intensify it almost to ecstasy." Clearly, as the QAnon phenomenon has made saliently obvious, social media have provided liars, like never before, with the means to intensify the ecstasy of the illusion of knowledge.

7

THE COGNITIVE LINGUISTIC PERSPECTIVE

Prologue

The goal of the present book has been to discuss and illustrate how a cognitive linguistic perspective can help decode the language of politically motivated lies and conspiracy theories. The premise on which it is based is that metaphorical framing is what makes these falsehoods believable, since the frames affect cognition and beliefs in an unconscious way. This chapter looks at this premise in a summary way, ending with implications for turning off the mental switches that metaphor activates. As discussed throughout, this perspective was used by Lakoff to examine political discourse in general. The focus here has been on the ways in which metaphor has been used by nefarious political actors in a manipulative way.

The master strategy that guides the big liar is to sow division through rhetoric—creating an "us-versus-them" dichotomy intended to bring down the existing social system through division. Around this core image schema of division into opposing groups, the political manipulator derives his many interconnected metaphorical frames designed to further enlarge the division. As Lakoff has shown, there really is no such thing as liberal or conservative politics, just discourses that are ensconced in particular metaphorical constructs that can take any political form—after all, Mussolini came forth to promote freedom of thought, as did Trump. The truly effective big liars founded their own political systems, such as Nazism and Fascism, on the basis of their metaphorical and false mythological strategies. These were grounded on a self-serving master metaphor, not on any allegiance to any historically-established political ideology. Indeed, the movements that big liars initiated have been labeled as everything from liberal socialism to totalitarian communism. The only "politics" that the political manipulator accepts is his own, which he achieves by divisive metaphorical language. The term *politics* was introduced by Aristotle, which he used to

DOI: 10.4324/9781003349143-7

describe collective behavior in a society based on a system of beliefs. At a surface level, Aristotle defined it as the "affairs of cities;" at a deeper level, however, he saw it as the practice of influencing people to subscribe to a particular system of collective governance with the use of rhetorical discourse. Without such discourse, there would be no politics, just an instinctive form of group interaction based on a desire for harmony and conformity.

Early on the Greeks realized that the arts of lying and deception would shape politics, and even be seen as an intrinsic part of the game of politics, constituting a common mode of strategic human interaction (Meilbauer 2018). However, they also realized that it could be used for good, dividing politics into ethical and unethical forms, described as democratic and demagogic respectively. Examining the primary strategies of demagoguery was seen by the Greek philosophers and writers as central to grasping how political power is gained and exercised by manipulating people's minds. As one of India's twentieth-century philosophers, Sri Auribondo, put it in 1918 (in Auribondo 2000) politics and discourse are intrinsically intertwined: "The shifty language of politics ... that strange language full of falsities of self-illusion and deliberate delusion of others, which almost immediately turns all true and vivid phrases into a jargon, so that men may fight in a cloud of words without any clear sense of the thing they are battling for."

The Central Problem

Resolving the central strategy of political demagoguery—the us-versus-them one—is through an approach in which the two sides, usually labeled as conservative and liberal, are shown to have contradictory worldviews expressed through differentiated central metaphors. As Lakoff has claimed, the political differences in America are shaped by the central fatherhood metaphor (discussed previously), which is grounded in the image schema of the nation as a family; that is, Americans metaphorically understand their country as a family, with the government corresponding to the parents and the individual citizens corresponding to the children. It is one's belief in how a family is best organized that will have direct implications for the kind of politics adopted by individuals. As discussed, conservatives adopt the "strict father" image schema, while liberals tend to adopt the image schema of the "nurturing (nurturant) parent," without a figure head. Lakoff argues that progressive politics correspond to the nurturant parent metaphor, with the government ensuring that citizens are protected and assisted to achieve their potential; conservative politics, on the other hand, correspond to the strict father model, which expects the citizenry to behave in such a way that they must earn their stay. In this mind frame the nation needs a strong, dominant father figure to run the government, with his children (citizens) made into responsible adults (moral, patriotic, self-financing citizens), at which point the father (government) should stay out of their business. In contrast, in the nurturant parent model, both mothers and fathers work to keep the children away from corrupting influences (pollution, social injustice, poverty, etc.) by controlling or taming them through legislation. Now, while most Americans accept a blend of both metaphors, at different times, political speeches work primarily by invoking and urging the adoption of one or the other. The problem comes when a manipulator like Trump comes forth to use the father-based metaphor to his own advantage, taking on the role of the political father in the eyes of his followers.

The analytical deconstruction process, therefore, inheres in identifying how the central metaphor in political discourses is coopted and exploited by the demagogue. Needless to say, the control of metaphor for political reasons has always been the case in America, long before Trump, even for worthy causes (as we saw with Luther King's dream speech). The *journey* image schema, for example, has always been a central one used by politicians on all sides of the ideological continuum. One politician who used it masterfully was FDR (Franklin Delano Roosevelt). Below are some examples (from Wikimedia):

> My aim in taking this step is to establish and maintain continuous control.

> We are on our way and we are headed in the right direction.

> Step by step we have created all the government agencies necessary.

> The electorate of America wants no backward steps taken.

> With this change in our moral climate and our rediscovered ability to improve our economic order, we have set our feet upon the road of enduring progress.

> In the German and Italian peoples themselves there is a growing conviction that the cause of Nazism and Fascism is hopeless—that their political and military leaders have led them down the bitter road which leads not to world conquest but to final defeat.

The reason why even a single metaphor works is because it is not a word in semantic isolation, but part of a conceptual system of thought. In an expression such as *candy is sweet* we can easily detach *sweet* from the phrase and define it literally as "having a pleasant taste." It is when the word is combined with an abstraction such as *love*—*love is sweet*—that metaphorical meaning crystallizes. This conceptual metaphor implies that love and sweetness implicate each other—as in "She's my sweetheart;" "I love my honey;" and so on. Moreover, it is a cultural key to understanding why chocolates are given to a loved one on Valentine's Day, why romantic love is ritualized at a wedding ceremony by the eating of a cake, and so on. This suggests an interrelationship between cognition, culture, and metaphor. The central metaphor here is that of *love as nourishing food*. This comes out concretely in Chagga, a Bantu society of Tanzania, where the male in courtship situations is conceived as an eater and the female as his sweet food, as can be detected in expressions that mean, in translated form, "Does she taste sweet?" "She tastes sweet as sugar honey" (Emantian 1995). These are not exceptional and purely poetic utterances; they are the rule in courtship discourse, substantiating the premise that at various levels, including the cultural one, metaphor plays a dominant role. They also suggest that metaphorical interpretation is not an option. If contextual information is missing from an utterance such as the two paraphrases of the Chagga utterances above, and even not knowing the language, our inclination is to interpret it metaphorically, not literally.

This view of a "central metaphor" guiding thought in a specific conceptual domain, with derived metaphors delivering its cognitive force through discourse, was actually detected in the latter part of the nineteenth century by the German linguist-physiologist Wilhelm Wundt (1901), with his experiments on the processing of speech, followed by Karl Bühler (1908), who found that the recall of a given proverb was statistically higher if it was linked to a second proverb. Bühler concluded that metaphorical-connective thinking produced an effective retrieval form of memory and was, therefore, something to be investigated further in contrast to literal recall. Research has since corroborated this finding. It has also shown that metaphor activates inferential processes, suggesting that something can only be inferred by relating it to the meaning of something else to which it is, or can be, associated. There simply is no such thing as an "absolute abstract concept." There are mainly metaphorized ones. It was Charles Peirce who emphasized that many, if not most, of our originating concepts are formed by a type of inferential process that he called *abduction*. He described it as follows (Peirce 1931–1958, V: 180):

> The abductive suggestion comes to us like a flash. It is an act of *insight*, although of extremely fallible insight. It is true that the different elements of the hypothesis were in our minds before; but it is the idea of putting together what we had never before dreamed of putting together which flashes the new suggestion before our contemplation.

In effect, once a metaphor is used effectively it imprints itself into the mind as truth, as Nietzsche understood (Chapter 1). The very fact that even discussions about metaphor are, *necessarily*, based in metaphors themselves bears this out. As Edie (1976: 193) has appropriately remarked, it is "impossible to understand the human mind or human behavior except by making a metaphorical detour."

In effect, if liberals are to understand how conservatives think, and vice versa, they will have to understand their respective utilizations of central metaphors. Needless to say, not all those in a specific political camp think the same way. However, the central metaphor, and how it is verbalized, lies right below the surface of political consciousness and can be activated by an opportunistic form of oratory. Understanding the deeply rooted metaphorical frames might perhaps allow participants in the polity to enter into a veritable dialogue. However, once a master liar comes onto the scene, the use of big lies clouds consciousness and plunges people into divided conceptual territories. Metaphors are not just communicative devices; they influence the way we think and act.

What is particularly sinister in the liar's discourse repertoire is blaming the very victims that his lies aim to attack. Hitler, for instance, claimed fallaciously and deceptively that the big lie technique had been used by Jews to blame Germany's loss in World War I on German general Erich Ludendorff, who was a prominent nationalist political leader in the Weimar Republic. This was clearly intended to turn sentiment against the Jews and to justify the Holocaust, allowing Hitler to assert that he had a right to annihilate the Jews in self-defense—the same war defense metaphorical mechanism employed a little later by Lenin as we saw previously. As Hitler realized, repetition is critical, understanding that his actual big lie of racial superiority worked through indoctrination, becoming its own evidence base, given that through blends of metaphorical frames it becomes integrated into cognition in general.

Neural Circuitry

The reason why metaphors are powerful tools of persuasion is that they structure thought by mapping processes, making it easy to focus on certain things and ignore others. They do so by activating neural circuits as Lakoff and others have shown (for example, Feldman 2006). Using the image schema of the mind as a device, the notion of "switches" in the mind has been used throughout this book for descriptive convenience. The relevant research actually supports the view that metaphor produces the Korzybski effect and false narratives the Da Vinci Code effect—a way of indicating that metaphor activates neural circuitry and that when this happens it is almost impossible to turn the switch off (to be discussed further below). In a nutshell, this means that when we come across a big lie or a conspiracy theory, it can shape our ideas without us being aware of it. By being exposed to particular sinister metaphors, we may develop hostile feelings towards specific groups. This is why hate groups use the metaphorical strategy to turn the switches on, so as to motivate people to violent activism.

A salient example of the latter occurred in August of 2017, when groups of white supremacists arrived in the college town of Charlottesville to participate in a "Unite the Right" rally, protesting the removal of a statue of the Confederate general Robert E. Lee. The demonstration quickly turned violent, as clashes broke out between the white supremacists and counter-demonstrators who waited for them at the scene. The American media outlet, Vice News, followed the white supremacists throughout the escalation of the events. In the documentary *Charlottesville: Race and Terror*, some of the participants of the "Unite the Right" rally spoke before, during, between, and after the violent demonstrations. The documentary revealed that the "uniting" idea was grounded on all kinds of metaphors of hate. The protesters claimed that they were fighting against the "parasitic class of anti-white vermin" and the "anti-white, anti-American filth." One speaker said: "And, at some point, we will have enough power that we will clear them from the streets forever, that which is degenerate in white countries will be removed." These metaphors turned on mental switches in both groups of protesters, for unification of the right and against white supremacist speech and ideologies—generating hatred toward each other and ending in violent tragedy, with the death of one of the protesters against the white supremacists.

The key notion in decoding politically motivated lies is to examine the very same mechanisms that are used in ordinary (non-mendacious) speech, as has been done throughout this book, since speech of any kind is grounded in these mechanisms (Gibbs 2017; Kövecses 2020). What is especially crucial to note is that as source domains literally pile up in a genre of speech, each one connected to the others, the content appears meaningful in itself, and does not need any outside empirical evidence to justify it. For example, conceptual metaphors delivering the notion of *ideation* (how ideas, theories, and other such abstract constructs are understood) include the following source domains: *vision* ("I cannot see what you are saying"), *geometry* ("The ideas of Plato and Descartes are parallel in many ways"), *plants* ("That theory has deep roots in philosophy"), *buildings* ("Your theory is well constructed"), *food* ("That is an appetizing idea"), *fashion* ("His theory went out of style years ago"), and *commodities* ("You must package your ideas differently"). These form a network of source domains that cluster around the same target domain, onto which they are mapped and distributed, as in a circuit. So, it is not a single metaphor that turns on the switch, but the circuit in which it exists. The same circuitry is utilized by nefarious political liars to generat hatred of others, as for example *plants* ("They must be weeded out of society"), *buildings* ("The foreigners will knock down everything we have built"), *food* ("The foreigners must be vomited as bad food"), and so on. As, Lakoff (2014) has argued, based on relevant neuro-scientific evidence, the power of metaphor exists literally in the structure of the brain's circuitry in which metaphor is formed and structured. As he notes:

- The brain contains metaphor mapping circuits.
- These link distinct brain regions, integrating patterns from one circuit to another.
- Each circuit carries specific metaphorical content (source domain schemas), corresponding to real-world physical and social experiences.
- Where the experiences are the same culturally, the mappings tend to be the same.
- Complex metaphorical thought (such as the derivational processes discussed above and throughout this book) is formed via a neural binding mechanism, so that it appears to the brain to be a single Gestalt.
- Metaphorical inferences arise via the activation of metaphor mapping circuits.
- The activation of neural circuits spreads out from each neuron along existing pathways, creating links that get stronger as regular firing continues.
- Eventually, some links become "hard-wired," becoming more and more difficult to undo.

Lakoff's overall neural model is somewhat comparable to the one put forth by the present author previously (Danesi 2000, 2003). As an example, consider the word *tail*, which the dictionary defines as "the flexible appendage found at the rear end of an animal's body." This is the literal meaning of *tail* in utterances such as the following:

> My cat's *tail* is over one foot long.
> Are there any species of dogs without *tails*?
> That horse's *tail* is rather short, isn't it?

This meaning can be located in a separate literal network in which *tail* exists as a focal node, branching out to other nodes in the circuit, such as *appendage* and *rear-end*. These provide basic information about what a *tail* is—an extremity—and where it is found on an animal—on its rear end. These circuits then become connected to metaphorical ones which guide the extension of *tail* to encompass meanings such as the following:

> The *tail* of that shirt is not bleached.
> Do you want heads or *tails* for this coin toss?
> The *tail* section of that airplane is making a funny noise.

Such extensions are hardly random or disconnected from the original circuit. Shirts, coins, and airplanes are inferred in English-speaking cultures as having appendages or rear ends. So, through metaphorical inference these are interlinked to the *tail* network, which is how blending arguably works:

- Linkages in network circuitry show nodes crisscrossing, which can form blends as a metaphor is employed.
- Crisscrossing is, in fact, a salient characteristic of blending.
- The result is a meaning that activates the different parts of the brain, (metaphorically) turning them on.

This neural model can be used to explain why it is not the literal meaning of *snake* in an expression such as "The politician is a snake," but rather its metaphorical meaning that is processed—when the literal snake circuit crisscrosses the human (politician) circuit, it switches on the relevant metaphorical meaning. This goes on all the time, even when a word is used with literal intent. This was brought out dramatically by an event experienced by American linguist Benjamin Lee Whorf, when he worked as a fire prevention engineer in the late 1920s. The event occurred during one of his inspection visits to a plant where he noticed the workers carrying out tasks in a careful and cautious way inside a room with full gasoline drums, avoiding the smoking of cigarettes, while in another room, which had empty gasoline drums, labeled *Empty*, they were less careful, smoking thoughtlessly. The workers were clearly unaware of the danger that this posed, since someone might flick a cigarette stub into one of the empty drums, which would cause an explosion. This incident impressed upon Whorf that the behaviors of the workers were likely induced by the *Empty* labels on the drums, which influenced how they perceived the situation—namely, as harmless. He explained his assessment as follows (Whorf 1956: 135):

Around a storage of what are called 'gasoline drums,' behavior will tend to a certain type, that is, great care will be exercised; while around a storage of what are called 'empty gasoline drums,' it will tend to be different—careless, with little repression of smoking or of tossing cigarette stubs about. Yet the 'empty' drums are perhaps the more dangerous, since they contain explosive vapor. Physically, the situation is hazardous, but the linguistic analysis according to regular analogy must employ the word 'empty,' which inevitably suggests a lack of hazard.

This anecdote shows that human beings rarely perceive reality directly (that is through the senses and the instincts); rather, that they perceive it through language (and other sign systems). There is, of course, an instinctive sense of danger in all humans, regardless of the language they speak. But this sense can be turned off or on by human-made signs. The gasoline drum incident shows how it was easily turned off by a mere word label, which impelled the workers to *think* that the drums were harmless, because of the word's meaning as "containing nothing." It was that meaning that was mapped onto the situation, obscuring the danger that the drums actually posed.

A simple neural model that can be used to explain the location of the two types of circuits—literal and metaphorical—is the *bimodal* one, developed to explain the cognitive flow of information from the right to the left hemisphere (Danesi 2003). Bimodality implies that the right hemisphere of the brain is where metaphor is first encoded, and then transferred in meaning to the left hemisphere to give it stability as a concept. The essence of bimodality is encapsulated in Howard Gardner's (1982: 74) statement: "Only when the brain's two hemispheres are working together can we appreciate the moral of a story, the meaning of a metaphor, words describing emotion, and the punch lines of jokes." The brain takes in unfamiliar information via the experiential (probing) right-hemisphere functions to operate freely. So, during the initial stages of a political lie, this model suggests that the followers of the liar assimilate his input through the powerful emotional activities of the right hemisphere. As these are repeated over and over they congeal into left-hemispheric thought patterns, which organize the initial frames into stable units of meaning. At this point, they are no longer distinguishable as constructions of the liar, but as self-evident truths. As Sapolsky (2010) has aptly observed, the potential to manipulate behavior can be located in the "brain's literal-metaphorical confusions." He gives the example of hatred of the Tutsi tribe as an example:

Viscera and emotion often drive our decision making, with conscious cognition mopping up afterward, trying to come up with rationalizations for that gut decision. The viscera that can influence moral decision making and the brain's confusion about the literalness of symbols can have enormous consequences. Part of the emotional contagion of the genocide of Tutsis in Rwanda arose from the fact that when militant Hutu propagandists called for the eradication of the Tutsi, they iconically referred to them as "cockroaches." Get someone to the point where his insula activates at the mention of an entire people, and he's primed to join the bloodletting.

Turning the Switch Off

Decoding metaphorical speech as one of the sources of political mind manipulation (and arguably the most powerful one), the question becomes: Is there any way to turn the switch off, to extend the image schema of the mind as a device used in this book for convenience? Lakoff (2016) argues that to offset the effects of manipulative metaphorical lies, it is important to understand the metaphors of the other party and to self-examine one's own metaphors, which has been the overall objective of this book. To turn the switch off, he recommends deploying three main strategies:

Start with the truth. The first frame gets the advantage.
Indicate the lie. Avoid amplifying the specific language if possible.
Return to the truth. Always repeat truths more than lies.

There is no evidence, however, to suggest that linguistic and behavioral integrity will defeat the master Machiavellian liar. From Stalin to Trump the strategy has never worked. It took actual events, political and otherwise, to bring down the dictators. However, as Machiavelli himself suggested (paradoxically), one way to do so is to deceive the deceiver, a kind of Trojan Horse strategy. In effect, Machiavelli suggested to fight metaphor with metaphor, a strategy actually utilized by anti-Trump Republicans after he declared his presidential candidacy for the 2024 elections. Examples include William Barr's assertion that "Trump will burn down the GOP" (in Barr 2022). Perhaps by having served as Trump's Attorney General, Barr may have sensed that this was the only way to open people's eyes, or at the very least to enrage Trump. The *burn* metaphor activates a host of metaphorical circuits, including historical images of the burning of books, recalling the Nazi book bonfire of 1933. It links these image schemas effectively. The Republican governor of Maryland, Larry Hogan, used a baseball metaphor instead—which clearly reso-nates with a large swath of Americans—asserting that it was time to change the team manager given the many political losses that Trump had brought about, empha-sizing this with the derived metaphor of "three strikes and you're out" (in Olander 2022). And the previous governor of New Jersey, Chris Christie, remarked that Trump was a loser because he "puts himself before everybody else," evoking the impediment image schema rather effectively (in Papenfuss 2022).

Actually, Herman Melville, who alerted Americans to the danger of con artists, used a similar strategy of using metaphor to combat metaphor in his 1857 novel, *The Confidence Man: His Masquerade*. Outraged by the plethora of con men in

America, in business and politics, Melville's novel was designed as a cautionary tale about the social destruction that ensues when dishonest language becomes the basis of dealings among people. It recounts what happens when the devil boards a riverboat traveling down the Mississippi River. He goes unrecognized as the "evil one" because he is dressed in disguise, boarding the vessel to conduct shady business deals so as to inject evil into human affairs. In a culture of greed and rampant materialism, the con man is rarely recognized for who he really is, Melville suggests. His false claims are readily believed because of the false promises he makes, using guile, cunning, deviousness, and slyness to dupe ingenuous and naïve people to do his bidding. The moral of Melville's story is that the con man will eventually destroy America, since he has the keen ability to manipulate victims by gaining their confidence through the skillful telling of lies. Once entrapped by the huckster's web of lies and falsehoods, we are all inclined to give him our trust. In his second chapter, Melville lists expressions to use against the deceiver, which he calls "epitaphic comments, posted on the boat" and which he hopes will not be "ignored blissfully by the deceiver's next victim" (from Melville 1857):

Poor fellow!
Who can he be?
Casper Hauser.
Bless my soul!
Uncommon countenance.
Green prophet from Utah.
Humbug!
Singular innocence.
Means something.
Spirit-rapper.
Moon-calf.
Piteous.
Trying to enlist interest.
Beware of him.
Fast asleep here, and, doubtless, pick-pockets on board.
Kind of daylight Endymion.
Escaped convict, worn out with dodging.
Jacob dreaming at Luz.

Each is a self-explanatory metaphorical or ironic frame for understanding con artistry, which could potentially be used to warn people of the master liar in their midst. However, it is difficult to counteract deception with metaphorical warnings. In a perceptive article, Max Boot remarks with respect to Trump: "Voters knew what sort of huckster Trump was when they elected him. But it should give us pause to consider what it says about America, circa 2018, that so many of us are so ready to accept … a con man … as our leader."

A 2016 study on the effects of lying by Garrett et al. has made it obvious that once a lie is accepted as believable, the brain becomes susceptible to subsequent lying, making it easier for a master liar to spin all kinds of self-serving conspiracy narratives among his believers. By using scans that measured the brain's response to lying, the researchers noticed that each new lie resulted in smaller and smaller neurological reactions—especially in the amygdala, which is the brain's emotional core. The goal of this book has been to show that decoding political lies and conspiracies—no matter what political side of the fence one is on—is one way to block what can be called the fossilization of lies in the brain's amygdala, whereby truth and lies are no longer distinguishable. Using conceptual metaphor theory as a decodification tool, the source of the most persuasive lies, and thus the most dangerous, can be located and examined directly. Perhaps this kind of understanding in itself will allow a certain form of protection against the consummate liar. As Korzybski (1933) emphasized, we really cannot perceive reality directly; but through our language map, which charts it for us:

> Moreover, every language having a structure, by the very nature of language, reflects in its own structure that of the world as assumed by those who evolve the language. In other words, we read unconsciously into the world the structure of the language we use.

Korzybski believed that human understanding is constrained by two factors: the structure of the human nervous system, and the structure of human languages—the two mirror each other. So, people cannot experience the world directly, but only through a combination of nerve-sensory and linguistic processes. As Korzybski himself suggested, by studying the sources of falsehoods and then coming up with ideas for combatting them we might be able to counteract them.

Epilogue

Korzybski's map-territory metaphor has been used throughout this book as a kind of metaphorical lens through which political mendacity can be viewed—namely as the use of the same maps that people already have in their minds projecting them onto illusory territories that will seem more real than real. When the false maps take the form of big lies, the deflection away from reality is big as well.

All lies are deleterious to some extent, but some lies are more destructive than others, since they can affect mental and physical harmony, both of individuals and entire societies. The big lies of dictators and conspiracy theory groups affect all people negatively, no matter their political persuasion. In fact, the big liar can alter one's political allegiances, as was witnessed during the US 2016 presidential campaign when many Democrats voted for a Republican, Donald Trump. The big liar knows how to extricate politics from its traditional social landscape and twist it for his own self-serving ends. In fact, there is no real politics when new forms of governance, such as Nazism and Fascism, are literally constructed by the master liar.

There are many ways in which political demagoguery can be anatomized, as has been done across time (see Meilbauer 2018). The premise adopted here is that cognitive linguistics provides a particularly insightful way in which to carry out the anatomy. The term "anatomy" is used here intentionally because a big lie will affect mental and bodily processes directly. As the dog biscuits anecdote discussed in this book (preface) has shown indirectly, words can affect us mentally and physically. Big lies do so in negative ways. So, like a mental or physical disease, we must first understand the anatomical (conceptual) structures that brought it about, before seeking remedies or antidotes against it.

Strategic fakery can inculcate certain beliefs that become congealed in people, leading to political activism, as the biggest lies of history have shown. The problem is that the metaphorical substratum on which they are forged is unconscious and derived from the history of a language. It is invisible to the conscious mind, and so it is felt to be inherently valid. This might explain why it puts up a mental shield against contrasting facts, inducing believers to ignore them, downplay them, or even turn them on their heads to confirm false beliefs. For this reason, it is unlikely that people with strong convictions will change their minds about them, given that the lie has impelled them to connect dots according to its deceptive map. This is the main "symptom" of the apophenic disease, as it can be called (metaphorically). Other symptoms include the development of fear towards certain groups, leading to the adoption and dissemination of hateful metaphors against those who do not subscribe to the same map.

A constant point-of-reference in the debate of how to control conspiracy theories, big lies, and hate speech is the First Amendment to the American Constitution: "Congress shall make no law respecting an establishment of religion, or prohibiting the free exercise thereof, or abridging the freedom of speech, or of the press; or the right of the people peacefully to assemble, and to petition the Government for a redress of grievances." The right to speak out publicly or privately, through any medium of expression, including books, newspapers, magazines, radio, television, motion pictures, and electronic and digital documents is made possible by this amendment. It is seen as a basic right of any free society, without which, it is claimed, the vital role of seeking and spreading new knowledge and truth will be hampered. But it also allows many to spread falsities and hatred freely. This is why some governments place limits on this freedom fearing the power of words to spur people to act hatefully. Censorship goes back to ancient societies, where it was used as a means to regulate the moral and political behavior of citizens, and thus seen as a form of benevolent state control in the best interests of the people. In some democratic countries, the media voluntarily censor themselves. In these countries, there are laws aiming to block hateful ideas from gaining wide diffusion. But nothing can stop the spread of big lies, given the proclivity of the brain to seek them out to explain events as connected, that is, given the presence of apophenic systems in cognition. Censorship has never worked and never will. What is critical is determining *who's* big lies will be believed. Why was Hitler or Trump so successful in swaying people with their big lies? The answer seems to be provided, in some part, by cognitive linguistics—the master liars understood subconsciously that by mapping source domains that resonate with people onto their own target domains, they were able to penetrate through the filters that the mind puts up.

In 1946, Orwell wrote a classic essay on the seductions of propaganda, *Politics and the English Language*. His target was the euphemistic (metaphorical) language used by extreme left-wing and right-wing parties and governments. If people could be persuaded to accept the specific discourse frame adopted by one or the other, they would be susceptible to having their conception of reality altered by such discourse. The American scholar Harold Lasswell described the pattern of conceptualization in his 1927 work, *Propaganda Technique in World War I*, which, he claimed, affected people's politics, family relations, and general outlooks. He also prefigured the notion of conceptual metaphor by pointing out that the most effective type of rhetorical strategies were what he called "developmental constructions" (essentially conceptual metaphors), because they undergird the creation of belief in related "mythological constructions," which prefigured the concept of conspiracy theories:

> As propaganda, developmental constructions are mythology. But such constructions are not always or not only propaganda. If tentatively and critically held, they are means to the end of orientation. Hence developmental constructions are related both to method and to myth.

To conclude this book, it is useful to quote Ralph Waldo Emerson's warning about lies and deceptions. He also saw lies as a form of disease affecting everyone in society: "Every violation of truth is not only a sort of suicide in the liar, but is a stab at the health of human society" (in Emerson 2020).

REFERENCES

Aarøe, Lene (2011). Investigating Frame Strength: The Case of Episodic and Thematic Frames. *Political Communication* 28: 207–226.

Arendt, Hannah (1978). Interview. *The New York Review*, October 26. https://www.nybooks.com/articles/1978/10/26/hannah-arendt-from-an-interview/

Aristotle (1952). *Rhetoric*. In: W. D. Ross (ed), *The Works of Aristotle*, Vol. 11. Oxford: Clarendon Press.

Aristotle (2009). *Nichomachean Ethics*. Oxford: Oxford University Press. (Originally 350 BCE).

Augustine (1964). *On Free Choice of the Will*, translated by A. Benjamin and L. Hackstaff. London: Pearson. (Originally 388 CE).

Augustine (1994). *On Lying*, translated by H. Brown. Boston: Hendrickson Publishers. (Originally circa 195 CE).

Aurobindo, Sri (2000). *India's Rebirth: Out of the Ruins of the West: A Selection from Sri Aurobindo's Writings, Talks and Speeches*. Paris: Institut de Recherches Évolutives.

Baigent, Michael, Leigh, Richard, and Lincoln, Henry (1982). *The Holy Blood and the Holy Grail*. Jonathan Cape.

Barkun, Michael (2003). *A Culture of Conspiracy: Apocalyptic Visions in Contemporary America*. Berkeley: University of California Press.

Barr, William P. (2022). Trump Will Burn Down the GOP. Time for New Leadership. *Common Sense*, https://www.commonsense.news/p/bill-barr-trump-will-burn-down-the-gop

Barthes, Roland (1957). *Mythologies*. Paris: Seuil.

Barthes, Roland (1981). Theory of the Text. In: R. Young (ed.), *Untying The Text*, pp. 31–47. London: Routledge.

Bateson, William (1972). *Steps to an Ecology of Mind*. New York: Ballantine.

Baudrillard, Jean (1983). *Simulations*. New York: Semiotexte.

Ben-Ghiat, Ruth (2016). An American Authoritarian. *The Atlantic*, August 20, 2016. https://www.theatlantic.com/politics/archive/2016/08/american-authoritarianism-under-donald-trump/495263/

Berkowitz, Reed (2020). A Game Designer's Analysis of QAnon. *Medium*, September 30. https://medium.com/curiouserinstitute/a-game-designers-analysis-of-qanon-580972548be5

Birchall, Clare (2006). *Knowledge Goes Pop: From Conspiracy Theory to Gossip.* New York: Berg.

Black, Jeremy (1987). *The English Press in the Eighteenth Century.* London: Routledge.

Blumenbach, Johann Friedrich (1828). *The Elements of Physiology*, translated by John Elliotson. London: Longman.

Boorstin, Daniel (1962). *The Image: A Guide to Pseudo-Events in America.* New York: Vintage.

Boot, Max (2018). Trump Spent His Business Career Swindling People. Nothing's Changed. *Chicago Tribune*, www.chicagotribune.com/news/opinion/commentary/ct-donald-trump-business-scams-20180503-story.html

Bougher, Lori D. (2012). The Case for Metaphor in Political Reasoning and Cognition. *Political Psychology* 33: 145–163.

Boulenger, Véronique, Shtyrov, Yury, and Pulvermüller, Friedemann (2012). When Do You Grasp the Idea? MEG Evidence for Instantaneous Idiom Understanding. *NeuroImage* 59: 3502–3513.

Braitich, Jack (2021). QAnon's Afterlife: A Holy Civil War. *Counterpunch*, January 15, https://www.counterpunch.org/2021/01/15/qanons-afterlife-a-holy-civil-war/

Brown, Dan (2003). *The Da Vinci Code.* New York: Doubleday.

Brugger, Peter (2001). From Haunted Brain to Haunted Science: A Cognitive Neuroscience View of Paranormal and Pseudoscientific Thought. In: Houran and R. Lange (eds.), *Hauntings and Poltergeists: Multidisciplinary Perspectives.* North Carolina: McFarland & Company.

Bühler, Karl (1908). On Thought Connection. In: D. Rapaport (ed.), *Organization and Pathology of Thought*, pp. 81–92. New York: Columbia University Press, 1951.

Byrne, Richard (1995). *The Thinking Ape: Evolutionary Origins of Intelligence.* Oxford: Oxford University Press.

Carey, Kelly (2017). *Fake News: How Propaganda Influenced the 2016 Election: A Historical Comparison to 1930's Germany.* Wharton, New Jersey: Marzenhale Publishing.

Carroll, Lewis (1865). *Alice's Adventures in Wonderland.* London: Macmillan.

Carroll, Lewis (1871). *Through the Looking-Glass, and What Alice Found There.* London: Macmillan.

Carver, Terrell and Pikalo, Jernej (eds.) (2008). *Political Language and Metaphor: Interpreting and Changing the World.* New York: Routledge.

Chomsky, Noam (2002). *Media Control: The Spectacular Achievements Propaganda.* New York: Seven Stories Press.

Chomsky, Noam and Herman, Edward (1988). *Manufacturing Consent: The Political Economy of the Mass Media.* New York: Pantheon.

Cicero (1942). *De Oratore*, translated by E. W. Sutton and H. Rackham. Cambridge: Harvard University Press. (Originally 55 BCE).

Clifton, David F. (2017). Make Athens Great Again! *The Harvard Crimson*, https://www.thecrimson.com/article/2017/3/1/clifton-make-athens-great/

Cohn, Norman (1967). *Warrant for Genocide: The Myth of the Jewish World Conspiracy and the Protocols of the Elders of Zion.* London: Serif Books.

Conrad, Klaus (1958). *Die beginnende Schizophrenie. Versuch einer Gestaltanalyse des Wahns.* Stuttgart: Georg Thieme Verlag.

Danesi, Marcel (2000). *Semiotics in Language Education.* Berlin: Mouton de Gruyter.

Danesi, Marcel (2003). *Second Language Teaching: A View from the Right Side of the Brain.* Dordrecht: Kluwer.

Danesi, Marcel (2004). *Poetic Logic: The Role of Metaphor in Thought, Language, and Culture.* Madison: Atwood Press.

Danesi, Marcel (2021). *Linguistic Relativity Today*. New York: Routledge.

Dawkins, Richard (1976). *The Selfish Gene*. Oxford: Oxford University Press.

Defoe, Daniel (1742). *Journal of the Plague Year*. London: E. Nutt.

DePaulo, Bella M., Kashy, Deboarh A., Kirkendol, Susan E., Wyer, Melissa M., and Epstein, Jennifer A. (1996). Lying in Everyday Life. *Journal of Personality and Social Psychology* 70: 979–995.

Derks, Lucas and Hollander, Jaap (1996). *Essenties van NLP*. Utrecht: Servire.

Dreyfus, Alfred (1937). *Dreyfus: His Life and Letters*. London: Hutchinson.

Dunbar, Robin (1997). *Grooming, Gossip, and the Evolution of Language*. Cambridge, Mass.: Harvard University Press.

Dunlap, Knight (1944). The Great Aryan Myth. *The Scientific Monthly* 59: 296–300.

Edie, James M. (1976). *Speaking and Meaning: The Phenomenology of language*. Bloomington: Indiana University Press.

Ellul, Jacques (1965). *L'illusion politique*. Paris: Robert Laffont.

Emantian, Michele (1995). Metaphor and the Expression of Emotion: The Value of Cross-Cultural Perspectives. *Metaphor and Symbolic Activity* 10: 163–182.

Emerson, Ralph Waldo (2020). *Essays*, The Project Gutenberg EBook of Essays, by Ralph Waldo Emerson, https://www.gutenberg.org/files/16643/16643-h/16643-h.htm

Erasmus, Desiderius (1876). *Praise of Folly*. London: Reeves & Turner. (originally 1509),

Evans, Alfred B. (1993). *Soviet Marxism-Leninism: The Decline of an Ideology*. Westport, Connecticut: Greenwood.

Fauconnier, Gilles and Turner, Mark (2002). *The Way We Think: Conceptual Blending and the Mind's Hidden Complexities*. New York: Basic.

Feldman, Jerome (2006). *From Molecule to Metaphor: A Neural Theory of Language*. Cambridge: MIT Press.

Feldman, Jerome and Narayanan, Srinivas (2004). Embodied Meaning in a Neural Theory of Language. *Brain and Language* 89: 385–392.

Feldman, Karen S. (2001). Conscience and the Concealment of Metaphor in Hobbes's Leviathan. *Philosophy and Rhetoric* 34: 21–37.

Festinger, Leon (1957). *A Theory of Cognitive Dissonance*. Evanston: Row, Peterson.

Festinger, Leon, Riecken, Henry W., and Schachter, Stanley (1956). *When Prophecy Fails*. London: Printer & Martin.

Frégier, Honoré Antoine (1840). *Des classes dangereuses de la population dans les grandes villes et des moyens de les rendre meilleures*. Lausanne: J.-B. Baillière.

Gallagher, Robert L. (2001). Metaphor in Cicero's "De Re Publica." *The Classical Quarterly* 51: 509–519.

Gardner, Howard (1982). *Art, Mind, and Brain: A Cognitive Approach to Creativity*. New York: Basic.

Garrett, Neil, Lazzaro, Stephanie, Ariely, Dan, and Tali, Sharot (2016). The Brain Adapts to Dishonesty. *Nature Neuroscience* 19: 1727–1732.

Gavrilets, Sergey and Vose, Aaron (2006). The Dynamics of Machiavellian Intelligence. *Proceedings of the National Academy of Sciences of the United States* 103: 16823–16828.

Gentner, Dedre (1979). The Shift from Metaphor to Analogy in Western Science. In: Andrew Ortony (ed.), *Metaphor and Thought*, pp. 447–480. Cambridge: Cambridge University Press.

Gibbs, Raymond (2017). *Metaphor Wars: Conceptual Metaphors in Human Life*. Cambridge: Cambridge University Press.

Giroux, Henry (2016). Challenging Trump's Language of Fascism. *Truthput*, January 9, 2016, https://truthout.org/articles/challenging-trumps-language-of-fascism/

Gobineau, Joesph Arthur (1856). *The Moral and Intellectual Diversity of Races*. Philadelphia: J. P. Lippincott.

Gramsci, Antonio (1947). *Lettere dal carcere*. Torino: Einaudi.

Grice, Herbert Paul (1975). Logic and Conversation. In: P. Cole and J. Morgan (eds.), *Syntax and Semantics*, Vol. 3, pp. 41–58. New York: Academic.

Grice, Herbert Paul (1989). *Studies in the Way of Words*. Cambridge: Harvard University Press.

Guldin, Rainer (2002). The dis-membered Body: Bodily Fragmentation as a Metaphor for Political Renewal. *Physis* 12: 10.1590/S0103-73312002000200003

Haimowitz, Ian (2020). No One is Immune: The Spread of Q-anon Through Social Media and the Pandemic, Center for Strategic and International Studies, https://www.csis.org/blogs/technology-policy-blog/no-one-immune-spread-q-anon-through-social-media-and-pandemic

Hanne, Michael, Crano, William D., and Scott Mio, Jeffery (eds.) (2014). *Warring with Words: Narrative and Metaphor in Politics*. Oxfordshire: Psychology Press.

Harper, David (2008). The Politics of Paranoia: Paranoid Positioning and Conspiratorial Narratives in the Surveillance Society. *Surveillance & Society* 5: 10.24908/ss.v5i1.3437.

Harris, Sam (2011). *Lying*. Encino: Four Elephants Press.

Hart, Joshua and Graether, Molly (2018). Something's Going on Here: Psychological Predictors of Belief in Conspiracy Theories. *Journal of Individual Differences* 39: 229–237.

Heine, Heinrich (1821). *Almansor: Eine Tragödie*. Project Gutenberg, https://www.gutenberg.org/ebooks/45600

Herder, Johann Gottfried (1770). *Abhandlungen über den Ursprung der Sprache*. Berlin: Chriftian Friedrich Voß.

Herman, Edward S. (1992). *Beyond Hypocrisy: Decoding the News in an Age of Propaganda Including A Doublespeak Dictionary for the 1990s*. Montreal: Black Rose Books.

Hermanowicz, Erika T. (2018). Augustine on Lying. *Speculum* 93. 10.1086/698318

Hitler, Adolph (1925). *Mein Kampf*. Munich: Franz Eher Nachfolger.

Hobbes, Thomas (1651). *Leviathan*. London: Andrew Crooke.

Hobbes, Thomas (1656). *Elements of Philosophy*. London: Molesworth.

Hobbs, Dick and Antonopoulos, Giorgios A. (2013). Endemic to the Species: Ordering the 'Other' Via Organised Crime. *Global Crime* 14: 27–51.

Hofstadter, Richard (1964). The Paranoid Style in American Politics. Harper Magazine, https://harpers.org/archive/1964/11/the-paranoid-style-in-american-politics/

Honeck, Richard P. and Hoffman, Robert R. (eds.) (1980). *Cognition and Figurative Language*. Hillsdale, NJ: Lawrence Erlbaum Associates.

Huxley, Aldous (1934). *Beyond the Mexique Bay*. London: Paladin.

Icke, David (2007). *The David Icke Guide to the Global Conspiracy*. Toronto: APG Books.

Irving, Clive (2018). Trump's War on the Press Follows the Mussolini and Hitler Playbook," *Daily Beast*, https://www.thedailybeast.com/trumps-war-on-the-press-follows-the-mussolini-and-hitler-playbook

James, William (1890). *The Principles of Psychology*. New York: Henry Holt.

Jaynes, Julian (1976). *The Origin of Consciousness in the Breakdown of the Bicameral Mind*. Boston: Houghton Mifflin.

Jimenez, Tyler, Arndt, Jamie, and Landau, Mark J. (2021). Walls Block Waves: Using an Inundation Metaphor of Immigration Predicts Support for a Border Wall. *Journal of Social and Political Psychology* 9: 159–171.

Johnson, Mark (1987). *The Body in the Mind: The Bodily Basis of Meaning, Imagination, and Reason*. Chicago: University of Chicago Press.

Joseph, John (2006). *Language and Politics*. Edinburgh: Edinburgh University Press.

Jowett, Garth and O'Donnell, Victoria (2005). *What Is Propaganda, and How Does It Differ From Persuasion?*. London: Sage.

Jung, Carl (1959). *The Archetypes and the Collective Unconscious*. Princeton: Princeton University Press.

Kafka, Franz (1915). *Die Verwandlung*. Leipzig: Kurt Wolff.

Kant, Immanuel (1790). *Critique of Pure Reason*. New York: St. Martin's.

King, Martin Luther (1965). Speech in Montgomery, Alabama (25 March 1965), transcribed from a tape recording.

Korzybski, Alfred (1921). *Manhood of Humanity: The Science and Art of Human Engineering*. New York: E. P. Dutton and Company.

Korzybski, Alfred (1933). *Science and Sanity*. Brooklyn: Institute of General Semantics.

Kövecses, Zoltán (2020). *Extended Conceptual Metaphor Theory*. Cambridge: Cambridge University Press.

Kristeva, Julia (1969) *Séméiotiké: Recherches pour un sémanalyse*. Paris: Seuil.

Kuper, Leo (1981). *Genocide: Its Political Use in the Twentieth Century*. New Haven: Yale University Press.

Kurila, Robin (2021). "Kung Flu"—The Dynamics of Fear, Popular Culture, and Authenticity in the Anatomy of Populist Communication. *Frontiers in Communication*, 10.3389/fcomm. 2021.624643

LaFrance, Adrienne (2020). The Prophecies of Q. *The Atlantic*, June 2020, https://www.theatlantic.com/magazine/archive/2020/06/qanon-nothing-can-stop-what-is-coming/610567/

Lakoff, George (1979). The Contemporary Theory of Metaphor. In: A. Ortony (ed.), *Metaphor and Thought*, pp. 202–251. Cambridge: Cambridge University Press.

Lakoff, George (1987). *Women, Fire, and Dangerous Things: What Categories Reveal about the Mind*. Chicago: University of Chicago Press.

Lakoff, George (2003). Metaphor and War, Again. *Language in Extreme Situations*, https://www.ugr.es/~jsantana/lies/metaphor_and_war_again.htm

Lakoff, George (2004). *Don't Think of an Elephant*. Chelsea, VT: Chelsea Green Publishing.

Lakoff, George (2008). *The Political Mind: Why You Can't Understand 21st-Century Politics with an 18th-Century Brain*. New York: Viking.

Lakoff, George (2014). Mapping the Brain's Metaphor Circuitry: Metaphorical Thought in Everyday Reason. *Frontiers in Human Neuroscience* 8: 10.3389/fnhum.2014.00958

Lakoff, George (2016a) *Moral Politics: How Liberals and Conservatives Think*, 3rd edition. Chicago: University of Chicago Press.

Lakoff, George (2016b). Understanding Trump. *Chicago University Press*, https://press.uchicago.edu/books/excerpt/2016/lakoff_trump.html

Lakoff, George (2017). Why Hate Speech Is Not Free Speech. https://george-lakoff.com/2017/09/08/why-hate-speech-is-not-free-speech/

Lakoff, George (2022). The Metaphor as Weapon. *Harvard Political Review*, https://harvardpolitics.com/metaphor-weapon/

Lakoff, George and Johnson, Mark (1980). *Metaphors We Live By*. Chicago: Chicago University Press.

Lakoff, George and Johnson, Mark (1999). *Philosophy in Flesh: The Embodied Mind and Its Challenge to Western Thought*. New York: Basic.

Langer, Walter C. (1972). *Mind of Adolf Hitler*. New York: Basic.

Lanier, Jaron (2010). *You Are Not a Gadget*. New York: Vintage.

Laswell, Harold (1927). *Propaganda Technique in World War I*. London: K. Paul, Trench, Trubner & Company.

Lenin, Vladimir (2011). *Speeches of Lenin: Voices of Revolt*. Literary Licensing, LLC. (October 15, 2011). Marxist Internet Archive, https://www.Marxists.org-lenin.

Lévi-Strauss, Claude (1962). *La pensée sauvage*. Paris: Plon.

Levy, Robert I. (1975). *Tahitians: Mind and Experience in the Society Islands*. Chicago: University of Chicago Press.

Lewandowsky, Stephan and Cook, John (2020). *The Conspiracy Theory Handbook*. http://sks.to/conspiracy

Lewental, Adam (2020). I Think Dan Brown Turned My Parents into QAnoners. *Salon*, https://www.salon.com/2020/12/18/qanon-conspiracy-dan-brown-da-vinci-code/

Lincoln, Abraham (1863). *The Gettysburg Address*. abrahamlincolnonline.org/lincoln/speeches/gettysburg.htm.

Linden, Sander van der (2015a). The Surprising Power of Conspiracy Theories. *Psychology Today*, August 24, https://www.psychologytoday.com/ca/blog/socially-relevant/201508/the-surprising-power-of-conspiracy-theories

Linden, Sander van der (2015b). The Conspiracy-Effect: Exposure to Conspiracy Theories (about Global Warming) Decreases Pro-social Behavior and Science Acceptance. *Personality and Individual Differences* 87: 171–173.

Linsroth, J. P. (2018). Myths on Race and Invasion of the Caravan Horde. *Counterpunch*, November 9, 2018. https://www.counterpunch.org/2018/11/09/myths-on-race-and-invasion-of-the-caravan-horde/

Lippmann, Walter (1913). *A Preface to Politics*. New York: Mitchell Kennerley.

Lippmann, Walter (1922). *Public Opinion*. New York: Macmillan.

Lund, Frederik H. (1925) The Psychology of Belief. *The Journal of Abnormal and Social Psychology* 20: 183–191.

Luther King, Martin (2020). *I Have a Dream in Its Entirety*. National Public Radio, https://www.npr.org/2010/01/18/122701268/i-have-a-dream-speech-in-its-entirety

Machiavelli, Niccolò (1513). *On Conspiracies*. Harmondsworth: Penguin, 2010.

Machiavelli, Niccolò (1532). *The Prince*, translated by W. K. Marriott. *The Project Gutenberg EBOOK of the Prince*, http://www.gutenberg.org/files/1232/1232-h/1232-h.htm

Mangiapane, Francesco (2018). The Discourse of Fake News in Italy. *Versus* 127: 291–306.

Marqués, Nestor (1900). *Fake News de la Antigua Roma*. Madrid: Espasa Calpe.

McCaskill, Nolan D. (2016). Trump Accuses Cruz's Father of Helping JFK's Assassin. *Politico*, politico.com/blogs/2016-gop-primary-live-updates-and-results/2016/05/trump-ted-cruz-father-222730

McLuhan, Marshall (1962). *The Gutenberg Galaxy: The Making of Typographic Man*. Toronto: University of Toronto Press.

McLuhan, Marshall (1964). *Understanding Media: The Extensions of Man*. Cambridge: MIT Press.

McLuhan, Marshall (1998). The Agenbite of Outwit, published posthumously in *McLuhan Studies* 1, Issue 2: 27.

Meerloo, Joost (1956). *The Psychology of Thought Control, Menticide, and Brainwashing*. New York: World Publishing Company.

Meilbauer, Jörg (ed.) (2018). *The Oxford Handbook of Lying*. Oxford: Oxford University Press.

Melville, Herman (1857). *Confidence-Man: His Masquerade*. London: Longman.

Merlan, Anna (2019). *Republic of Lies: American Conspiracy Theorists and Their Surprising Rise to Power*. New York: Metropolitan.

Meyer, Pamela (2010). *Liespotting*. New York: St. Martin's.

Milner, Ryan M. (2016). *The World Made Meme: Public Conversations and Participatory Media*. Cambridge: MIT Press.

Milton, John (1652). *Paradise Lost*. London: Samuel Simmons.

Mitnick, Kevin D. and Simon, William L. (2001). *The Art of Deception*. New York: Wiley.

Morris, Desmond (1969). *The Human Zoo*. London: Cape.

Moynihan, Daniel Patrick (2010). *Daniel Patrick Moynihan: A Portrait in Letter of an American Visionary*. New York: PublicAffairs.

Müller, Friedrich Max (1888). *Biographies of Words and the Home of the Aryas*. Kessinger Publishing Reprint, 2004.

Musolff, Andreas (2004). *Metaphor and Political Discourse*. New York: Palgrave.

Musolff, Andreas (2007). What Role Do Metaphors Play in Racial Prejudice? The Function of Antisemitic Imagery in Hitler's *Mein Kampf. Patterns of Prejudice* 41: 21–43.

Mussolini, Benito (2018). *Selected Speeches of Benito Mussolini*. Amazon Digital Services.

Mussolini, Benito (2020). *Mussolini as Revealed in his Political Speeches*, translated and edited by Barone Bernardo Quaranta di San Severino. London: J. M. Dent & Sons.

Neocleous, Mark (1997). *Fascism*. Minneapolis: University of Minnesota Press.

Nicaso, Antonio and Danesi, Marcel (2020). *Organized Crime: A Cultural Perspective*. London: Routledge.

Nietzsche, Friedrich (1873). *On Truth and Lies in a Nonmoral Sense*. CreateSpace Independent Publishing Platform (Aug. 24 2012). https://www.austincc.edu/adechene/Nietzsche %20on%20truth%20and%20lies.pdf

Northeast Arkansas Community College Library (2022). Fake News vs. Real News: The Danger of the Word "Fake," September 19, library.nwacc.edu/fakenews/danger

Nunberg, Geoff (2018). Why The Term 'Deep State' Speaks To Conspiracy Theorists. NPR, August 9, 2018. https://www.npr.org/2018/08/09/633019635/opinion-why-the-term-deep-state-speaks-to-conspiracy-theorists

Olander, Olivia (2022). 3 Strikes, You're Out: Larry Hogan Laments Trump's Election Record. *Politico*, https://www.politico.com/news/2022/11/13/larry-hogan-trump-election-record-00066633

Ortony, Andrew (ed.) (1979). *Metaphor and Thought*. Cambridge: Cambridge University Press.

Orwell, George (1946). *Politics and the English Language*. London: Kemp House.

Orwell, George (1949). *Nineteen-Eighty-Four*. New York: Harcourt, Brace, and Company.

Orwell, George (1968). *The Collected Essays*, Vol. 3, edited by Sonia Orwell and Ian Angus. London: Secker and Warburg.

Orwell, George (2017). *Orwell on Orwell*. London: Harvell Secker.

Osgood, Charles (1968). *Conservative Words and Radical Sentences in the Semantics of International Politics*. Champaign: University of Illinois Press.

Otieno, Raphael Francis, Owino, Francis Rew, and Attyang, Judith Miguda (2016). Metaphors in Political Discourse: A Review of Selected Studies. *International Journal of English and Literature* 7: 21–26.

Papenfuss, Mary (2022). He 'Put Himself Before Everybody Else': Chris Christie Calls On GOP To Dump Trump. *Huffington Post*, https://www.huffpost.com/entry/chris-christie-dump-trump-losing_n_6379e4bce4b06d5b60962c70

Paxton, Robert (2004). *The Anatomy of Fascism*. New York: Vintage.

Peirce, Charles S. (2014). *Illustrations of the Logic of Science*. Chicago: Open Court. (Originally 1877–1878).

Plato (1994). *Gorgias*, translated by Robin Waterfield. Oxford: Oxford University Press. (Originally 380 BCE).

Plato (2019). *Meno*. The Internet Classics Archive: classics.mit.edu/Plato/meno.html

Plato (2020). *Phaedrus*. Project Gutenberg, http://www.gutenberg.org/files/1636/1636-h/1636-h.htm, section 262 (originally 370 BCE).

Polidoro, Piero (2018). Post-Truth and Fake News: Preliminary Considerations. *Versus* 127: 189–206.

Pollio, Howard R., Barlow, Jack M., Fine, Harold J., and Pollio, Marilyn R. (1977). *The Poetics of Growth: Figurative Language in Psychology, Psychotherapy, and Education*. Hillsdale, NJ: Lawrence Erlbaum.

Postman, Neil (1992). *Technopoly: The Surrender of Culture to Technology*. New York: Alfred A. Knopf.

Proust, Marcel (1925). *Remembrance of Things Past*, Vol. 3. New York: Random House, 1981.

Putin, Vladimir (2022). Full Text: Putin's Declaration of War on Ukraine. *The Spectator*, February 24. https://www.spectator.co.uk/article/full-text-putin-s-declaration-of-war-on-ukraine/

Reddy, Michael J. (1979). The Conduit Metaphor: A Case of Frame Conflict in Our Language about Language. In: Andrew Ortony (ed.), *Metaphor and Thought*, pp. 284–310. Cambridge: Cambridge University Press.

Reiss, Benjamin (1999). P. T. Barnum, Joice Heth and Antebellum Spectacles of Race. *American Quarterly* 51: 78–107.

Robertson, Donald J. (2021). The Military Metaphor in Marcus Aurelius. *Medium*, https://medium.com/stoicism-philosophy-as-a-way-of-life/the-military-metaphor-in-marcus-aurelius-6c0d337300fe

Roudakova, Natalia (2017). *Losing Pravda*. Cambridge: Cambridge University Press.

Russell, Bertrand (1950). *Unpopular Essays*. New York: Simon & Schuster.

Sagan, Carl and Druyan, Ann (1992). *Shadows of Forgotten Ancestors: A Search for Who We Are*. New York: Random House.

Sapolsky, Robert (2010). This Is Your Brain on Metaphors. *New York Times*, https://archive.nytimes.com/opinionator.blogs.nytimes.com/2010/11/14/this-is-your-brain-on-metaphors/

Sauter, M. J. (2017). The Apophenic Machine: The Conspiratorial Mode and the Internet's Data Hoard Were Made for Each Other. *Real Life*, https://reallifemag.com/the-apophenic-machine/

Scott, Peter Dale (1993). *Deep Politics and the Death of JFK*. Berkeley: University of California Press.

Scott Mio, Jeffery (1996). *Metaphor, Politics, and Persuasion*. London: Psychology Press.

Shapiro, Michael (1984). *Language and Politics*. New York: New York University Press.

Shinar, Chaim (2018). Conspiracy Narratives in Russian Politics from Stalin to Putin. *European Review* 26: 648–660.

Silverman, Craig (2016). This Analysis Shows How Viral Fake Election News Stories Outperformed Real News On Facebook. *BuzzFeed News*, November 16. https://www.buzzfeednews.com/article/craigsilverman/viral-fake-election-news-outperformed-real-news-on-facebook

Smith, David Livingston (2004). *Why We Lie, The Evolutionary Roots of Deception and the Unconscious Mind*. New York: St. Martin's Press.

Sontag, Susan (1978). *Illness as Metaphor*. New York: Farrar, Straus & Giroux.

Sontag, Susan (1989). *AIDS and Its Metaphors*. New York: Farrar, Straus & Giroux.

Steen, Gerard (2015). Developing, Testing and Interpreting Deliberate Metaphor Theory. *Journal of Pragmatics* 90: 10.1016/j.pragma.2015.03.013

Tangherini, Timothy R., Shahsavari, Shadi, Shahbazi, Behnam, Ebrahimzadeh, Ehsan, and Roychowdhury, Vwani (2020). An Automated Pipeline for the Discovery of Conspiracy and Conspiracy Theory Narrative Frameworks: Bridgegate, Pizzagate and Storytelling on the Web, *PLoS ONE*: 10.1371/journal.pone.0233879.

Taylor, Kathleen (2004). *Brainwashing: The Science of Thought Control*. Oxford: Oxford University Press.

Tralau, John (2014). Deception, Politics and Aesthetics: The Importance of Hobbes's Concept of Metaphor. *Contemporary Political Theory* 13: 112–129.

Turner, Mark (1997). *The Literary Mind*. Oxford: Oxford University Press.

Turner, Mark and Fauconnier, Gilles (1995). Conceptual Integration and Formal Expression. *Metaphor and Symbolic Activity* 10: 183–204.

Waals, Frans de (1982). *Chimpanzee Politics*. Baltimore: Johns Hopkins University Press.

Wheeler, Tom (2021). The Legacy of Trump's Social Media Policy. *Brookings*, https://www.brookings.edu/blog/techtank/2021/03/15/the-legacy-of-trumps-social-media-content-policing/

Whorf, Benjamin Lee (1956). *Language, Thought, and Reality*. In J. B. Carroll (ed.). Cambridge, Mass.: MIT Press.

Wineburg, Sam, McGrew, Sarah, Breakstone, Joel, and Ortega, Teresa. (2016). Evaluating Information: The Cornerstone of Civic Online Reasoning. *Stanford Digital Repository*: http://purl.stanford.edu/fv751yt5934

Wooley, Richard (2018). Donald Trump, Alex Jones and the Illusion of Knowledge. CNN, August 6, 2018. https://www.cnn.com/2017/07/15/opinions/trump-alex-jones-world-problem-opinion-wooley/index.html

Wright, Richard (1995). *The Moral Animal: Why We Are the Way We Are*. New York: Vintage.

Wundt, Wilhelm (1901). *Sprachgeschichte und Sprachpsychologie*. Leipzig: Eugelmann.

Yin, Lijun and Weber, Bernd (2019). I lie, why don't you: Neural mechanisms of individual differences in self-serving lying. *Human Brain Mapping* 40: 1101–1113.

Yogerst, Chris (2021). Pseudo-Events in the 21st Century. *Los Angeles Review of Books*, https://lareviewofbooks.org/article/pseudo-events-in-the-21st-century/

Young, Kevin (2017). *Bunk: The Rise of Hoaxes, Humbug, Plagiarists, Phonies, Post-Facts, and Fake News*. Minneapolis: Graywolf.

Yu, Xing (2013). *Language and State: An Inquiry into the Progress of Civilization. United States of America*. Lanham: University Press of America.

INDEX

Printed in the USA
CPSIA information can be obtained
at www.ICGtesting.com
LVHW02052025 0823
756187LV00006B/545